Whispers from the Edge of Eternity

REFLECTIONS ON LIFE AND FAITH
IN A PRECARIOUS WORLD

CHARLES RINGMA

REGENT COLLEGE PUBLISHING
Vancouver, British Columbia

This edition published 2005 by Regent College Publishing
in association with the Piquant Agency
4 Thorton Road, Carlisle, CA3 9HZ U.K.

Regent College Publishing
5800 University Boulevard, Vancouver, BC V6T 2E4 Canada
Web: www.regentpublishing.com
E-mail: info@regentpublishing.com

Views expressed in works published by Regent College Publishing
are those of the authors and do not necessarily represent the official
position of Regent College <www.regent-college.edu>.

Unless otherwise noted, all Scripture quotations are from the
New International Version of the Bible,
copyright © 1973, 1978 by the International Bible Society.
Used by permission of Zondervan Publishers.

Library and Archives Canada Cataloguing in Publication

Ringma, Charles
Whispers from the edge of eternity / Charles Ringma.

ISBN 1-57383-325-8

1. Christian life—Meditations. 2. Prayer-books and devotions.
I. Title.

BV4501.3.R553 2004   242   C2004-905599-2

CONTENTS

Preface 9

Introduction 11

GRACE: Gifts of God's Generosity 13

FAITH: The Heart's True Home 27

TRUST: Experiencing Goodness 41

HOPE: Living in Anticipation 53

COMMUNITY: Sharing Life Together 65

HEALING: Growth in Wholeness 83

PRAYER: Echoes of the Longing Heart 97

ATTENTIVENESS: The Art of Contemplation 109

FORGIVENESS: Extending Grace 123

RELIQUISHMENT: Living with Open Hands 133

CALLING: Living Obedience 143

JOURNEYING: Following the God of Surprises 157

VULNERABILITY: Recognizing our Humanness 167

SERVICE: Living Love of Neighbor. 181

WITNESS: Sacraments for a Broken World 195

AN AFTERWORD 209

Scripture Index 212

Author Index 214

For
Peter and Dorothy Lane
ever involved in serving those at the margins

PREFACE

These reflections have not been written while I have been sitting on a mountain rapped in beautific adoration and prayer. This, of course, is not to say that I have not had moments and seasons, where in the blessing of contemplation, something of the ordinariness of the world was rolled back, and glimmers of the world to come shone more brightly. But such times are not the normal diet of my spiritual experience. Unfortunately, not. For if they were, I am sure that I could have lived more truly, more faithfully, more prophetically, and so more critically of the values and ethos of our age.

Instead, these reflections have mainly been written in the busy round of life: teaching, mentoring, involvement with the poor and seeking to serve God's people on several continents.

In the midst of these realities the blessing of God's presence, and the hope of the manifestation of God's fuller kingdom, have provided fuel for the journey. In the midst of this journey, these reflections have been written.

I am especially grateful to the Board of Governors of Regent College, who in the gift of a generous sabbatical, provided the space and time to bring this writing project to completion.

My special thanks to Marina Ringma-McLaren who translated my torturous handwriting into a typescript.

This book is meant to serve as a companion volume to *Life in Full Stride* published by Regent College Publishing, Vancouver and OMF Literature in Manila.

Charles Ringma
Brisbane, Vancouver, Manila, Yangon
2004

INTRODUCTION

I wish that I could say that with time everything becomes clearer and more certain. And that in walking the Christian journey one becomes more sure-footed the longer one is on the road.

I would like to say this because I hoped that this would be the case: that Christian spirituality is the singular journey from immaturity to greater wisdom and authenticity.

But this has not been my experience. Nor, it seems, is it the experience of others.

The Christian journey is far more complex that an evolutionary upward movement. There are strange contours in the road. There are the persistent paradoxes. And there is the mystery of faith.

But there is the certainty of the Word of God. And there is the reality of being touched by the transforming grace of God. And there is the blessing of the Christian community where our faith is nurtured. And there is the hope of new heavens and a new earth.

And there are the surprising experiences of grace where the heavens seem to open.

Henri Nouwen during his retreat at the Genesee Trappist Monastery speaks of such an experience: "during a few hours I felt that the presence of God was so obvious and my love for him so central that all the complexities of existence seemed to unite in one point and become very simple and clear" (*The Genesee Diary: Report from a Trappist Monastery,* New York: Doubleday, 1976, p. 121).

Over a decade later, after an accident and waking up from emergency surgery, Nouwen again had a taste of God's unconditional love and a sense of being "sent to make the all-embracing love of the Father known to people who hunger and thirst for love." He admits that soon afterwards he had "lost much of the peace and freedom that was given to me" (*Beyond the Mirror: Reflections on Death and Life*, New York: Crossroad, 1991, p. 59 and p. 72)

And so it may well be with us. Moments of bliss, and then the long struggle. Whispers from the edge of eternity, and then the long journey of faith.

The brighter colours, therefore, are not the whole picture. Faith also has its uncertainties, and our healing is far from complete. Moreover, we continue to live in a world where there is so much injustice.

While we may wish for an ever-present spiritual clarity and for an unquestioning certainty of faith, we are often called to walk a more difficult road. On this road it is often more a matter of being held in God's hand, than of holding God's hand.

Light has its shadows and grace has its pains. Joy is not without sorrow, and despair has the fragile veins of hope.

This meditational reader seeks to reflect something of this kind of textured picture of the Christian journey, and hence these are the whispers from the edge of eternity.

GRACE

GIFTS OF GOD'S GENEROSITY

A WIDE EMBRACE

This is a trustworthy saying that deserves full acceptance (and for this we labor and strive), that we have put our hope in the living God, who is the Savior of all men, and especially of those who believe.

1 Timothy 4:9-10

It matters little how clever, attractive or powerful we may be, we don't easily see ourselves as worthy of love. This is hardly surprising, since we are only too aware of our failures and weaknesses. And we are often affected by self-doubt.

Sadly, the notion persists that we somehow need to be worthy of love. We need to be deserving. And so frequently, we work at earning love by using our abilities or resources to gain the love we crave for.

The pattern to gain love in this way is frequently scripted in the rhythm of life in our family of origin where we eagerly strove to achieve in order to get parental approval and affection.

It is, therefore, hardly surprising that we take this unharmonious melody with us into other aspects of life and into other relationships. Not only are our romantic relationships seen in this light, but our friendship with God is also colored with the need to perform and to gain approval.

The remarkable message of the gospel, however, is that God's love in Christ is freely given out of God's beneficence and is not based on our performance.

As a result, the playing field has been leveled. We don't receive God's blessings because we are clever or powerful. We receive them because God is generous to all who come to him in humility, receptivity and repentance.

Thus there are no favorite people in God's scheme of things. Neither one's ethnicity nor one's status have a special place with God. God extends his love to all. And St. Irenaeus captures this well: "Christ on the cross, through his outstretched arms, seeks to embrace all people, from the East to the West."

The generous embrace of God is often full of surprises. Unlikely people are invited to sit at God's banquet table. Those who have little are given much. Those who never thought they were good enough are welcome.

Thus at the heart of the gospel is a welcome. That welcome issues in an embrace. And that embrace invites us to see ourselves and to live our life in the light of God's amazing love for us.

This love does not call us to a life of striving, but a life of service lived in thankfulness to the God of all grace.

Reflection: What are the implications of living out of the generous love of God?

THE WIDE AND DEEP PLACES

Come, all you who are thirsty, come to the waters; and you who have no money, come, buy and eat! Come, buy wine and milk without money and without cost.

Isaiah 55:1

It is true that *spirituality* is not only about special experiences. Spirituality is experiencing the presence, grace and goodness of God in the ordinary rhythms and events of life. As such, we can speak of a spirituality of everyday life. Thus God is as intrinsic to our Mondays as to our Sundays.

But in saying this, we must not limit God to our Mondays. The more prosaic rhythms of life should not be made normative for our existence. There is more to life than only its often monotonous routines, and its daily responsibilities and duties. Furthermore, while God's presence should be sought in these routines, there is more to life than its regularities, and God will always be the God of surprises.

Teilhard de Chardin once remarked "by means of that divine thirst, which is your gift, the access to the great waters may open wide within you." That we long for more than the routines of life is everywhere evident. The massive entertainment industry is but one indicator of that fact. That we seek the transcendent is also a marker of our humanity. The human quest for some form of deeper spirituality continues.

But that deep things would open up for us, that we would end up in wide spaces, is an invitation to explore the vapor trails and the flashes of light of the Divine Spirit. The reservoirs within the caverns of our being are not simply the places of our own making. They are residual gifts of God that need to be fanned into flame.

I have deliberately mixed the images in the above paragraph in talking about water and fire. These were seen as the primal forces of the ancient world. This terminology is also woven into the biblical story. But at heart, these are signs of the life-giving Spirit. Living Water. The purging fire of the Spirit. Baptism in water. Baptism in the Holy Spirit.

Everywhere in the biblical narrative there are the word pictures of life opening within us, and the Spirit descending upon us. Wells spring open within us, and the rain of God is poured out upon us. Thus both the movements within and without are the blessings that come our way from God's generous hand.

So how may things open wide within us, and how may we come to these wide places? How can the deep wells burst open, and the gentle rains fall upon our head? How does the fire of God enflame us? And how are we renewed and empowered?

While the answer at the most fundamental level is that these things are hidden in the mystery and surprises of God, there are some indicators. It does have to do with the seeking and longing heart, as much as the sovereignty of God. It does have to do with the places of pain and transition, as much as with the surprises of God. And it does have to do with the deep dissatisfactions in our lives, as much as the renewing presence of the Holy Spirit.

The waters of life can well up within the sanctuary and in the ordinary activities of our lives. In all the dimensions of life God longs to be present and draw us into wide spaces.

Reflection: In what ways can I be more open to the strange work of God in my life, my relationships and my world?

GOD, THE GIVER OF
ALL GOOD THINGS

*But we ought always to thank God for you, brothers loved by the Lord,
because from the beginning God chose you to be saved through the
sanctifying work of the Spirit and through belief in the truth.*

2 Thessalonians 2:13

Our contemporary culture operates on the basis that we
urgently need more in order to be truly happy. Christian
good news operates on the basis that we have already received so
much in God that we can be truly thankful.

Moreover, our contemporary values seem to suggest that we
need more things in order to be fulfillled. These things are a
whole range of consumer products. In contrast, the gospel speaks
of the importance of relationships in making life rich. These
relationships with God, family, friends, and the wider community
are what make life full and joyful.

What this suggests is that the gospel is on a serious collision
course with contemporary values. And long gone are the days
when Christian values were generally held by the wider general
culture.

There are several challenges in all of this. The first, is that
Christians cannot expect to receive help in their journey of faith
from the wider society. As a result, they have to dig deeper so they
may drink from their own wells. Put differently, Christians need

to be more deeply embedded in Scripture and a life of prayer in order to resist the idolatries of their age.

The second challenge, is to share the gospel with others so that they may know the God who in the face of Jesus Christ has brought salvation and hope. And that through the power of the gospel they may be able to overcome the crippling values of our age. Values which have made personalism a poor second to productivity.

The issues that face us as contemporary Christians are too much for us. In our own strength we cannot rise up and respond to these challenges. We need God's presence and grace more fully in our lives, and we need to give ourselves more fully to the God who calls us.

This is nowhere put more clearly than in the words of Bernard of Clairvaux: "in his first work [of creation] he gave me myself; in his second work [of redemption] he gave me himself. When he gave me himself, he gave me back myself. Given and regiven, I owe myself twice over."

The God of the Bible has not only given us the earth as his generous gift, but also his very self in Jesus Christ. God is the giver of all good things and we are welcomed to become the happy recipients of his grace. And out of this grace we can live a very different life to what our culture offers. Thus we live to God's glory and as a blessing to others.

Reflection: What effect could a life of receptivity and deep thankfulness have?

WINESKINS

Neither do men pour new wine into old wineskins. If they do, the skins will burst, the wine will run out and the wineskins will be ruined. No, they pour new wine into new wineskins, and both are preserved.

Matthew 9:17

There is an old Tibetan saying which has a similar ring to the Matthean passage: "the milk of the lioness is so precious and so powerful that if you put it in an ordinary cup, the cup breaks."

This verse in Matthew has often been applied to renewal movements in the life of the church. The logic operating in this historical perspective is basic enough: when the Spirit renews the members of the community of faith, this will lead to new church structures.

But while this may be a valid application of the verse, this passage is not talking first of all about the renewal of the church. It is talking about the in-breaking of the Kingdom of God. It speaks of God's action and reign. It speaks of the new life that God brings which calls for receptivity and change.

There is little doubt that we humans have been given many and wonderful abilities. The gift of creativity and innovation are part of the human story. And everywhere around us are the signs of human ingenuity. And so we create families, institutions, cities, and cultures.

But even though so much of what we make and do is good, it does not approximate the banquet table of God's Kingdom. What

21

we do may benefit our life, but it does not quench our deepest thirst. It is water, but not wine.

The life that God gives through the in-breaking of his Kingdom is subversive and transformational. It shakes us loose from the familiar flow and patterns of our life. These patterns, while good, are often less than life-giving because they mask the idolatries that plague the human condition. Moreover, all that we create eventually falls into dissolution and becomes dysfunctional.

God's new wine thus disrupts the familiar quenching of our thirst and makes us aware of what we lack and need.

Having once eaten at God's banqueting table, having tasted the new wine of the Kingdom and having received the new life that God gives by his renewing Spirit, we will never be satisfied with anything less. Not even with what our religious institutions may wish to give us. For while these institutions are to be a sign and sacrament of God's renewing work in our lives, and in the world, they sometimes are not. They do become old and tired, and are affected by the ways of the world. Its members may have ceased to drink at the fountain of life for themselves.

Therefore, we all need to drink again and again. In our personal lives, in our families, in our churches and in our religious institutions we need the wind of the Spirit, the breath of God, the new life that God gives.

This gift of new life and renewal is not something we have to wrench from the hand of a reluctant God. God bends towards us in his generosity. But it is something we need to seek and hunger for.

Reflection: Where do I need the new wine of God?

EMPOWERING GRACE

For you know the grace of our Lord Jesus Christ, that though he was rich, yet for your sakes he became poor, so that you through his poverty might become rich.

2 Corinthians 8:9

It is a basic observation of life that often the elite and the powerful, while they may be involved in various forms of token giving, do not give anything significant away. Rather, they continue to hold and to accumulate.

Those of us who do not have much may roundly criticize them. But we are basically no different. We too seek power and want much.

It is, therefore, a total surprise that God who is all powerful and all possessing, is so radically different. From his generous hand come the gifts of creation and from his passionate heart comes the gift of his only Son.

Unlike the rich of our world who live in palatial isolation, cocooned in their prosperity, the God of the Bible enters the human fray to heal a wounded humanity, and bring deliverance to the oppressed and the poor.

Spilling over the pages of the sacred text we read of a God who comes down, who engages us in our brokenness, and who seeks our transformation and wholeness.

Nowhere do we see the downward mobility of God, and his willingness to embrace suffering, more clearly than in the self-giving of the Son in whom God was reconciling the world to himself.

Those of us who have been touched by this act of humiliation must never assume that God has blessed us merely for ourselves. God's empowering grace heals us so that we in turn can become the servants of others.

Dorothy Day whose conversion led her to serve the poor and to work for justice speaks of the blessing of "precarity." This speaks of the open hand rather than the closed fist, and relinquishment rather than holding and grasping. It speaks of an embrace of voluntary poverty that gives us the freedom to act on behalf of the poor.

All of this is so strange for us. We think that when we are powerful we have most to give, and when are in control we can best bless others. But in the action of God we see something very different. In the incarnation we see vulnerability. In Christ's life we see servanthood. And is his death we see utter humiliation. But the shameful cross leads to the resurrection that speaks of new life for all.

We who are blessed by Christ are also bound to Christ. His life becomes normative for us. We too are called to downward mobility, to servanthood, to precarity.

Reflection: Where does God's empowering grace need to pry me loose from securities that prevent me from living a life of following the Servant king, Jesus Christ?

TRANSFORMATION

But now that you have been set free from sin and have become slaves to God, the benefit you reap leads to holiness, and the result is eternal life. For the wages of sin is death, but the gift of God is eternal life in Christ Jesus our Lord.

Romans 6:22-23

Most of us have experienced some momentous events which have deeply moved us and possibly changed our lives forever. These events may have been tragic or deeply joyful. A family death, the devastation of property, the experience of war, a natural disaster, the pain of loss, and many other similar events may have impacted us so deeply that we will never be the same again.

Similarly, moments of joy and happiness can affect us profoundly. The birth of a child. The beauty of romance. The gift of friendship. The experience of care. The blessing of forgiveness and reconciliation. The joy of acceptance.

Just as in times of difficulty, so in times of joy, things can come our way that leave their mark upon our lives.

Niall Williams makes the observation that 'when something of great size moves into the heart it dislodges all else, in just the same way that the forward movement of the queen [in chess] reshapes the board'. And there is nothing so monumental that impacts us forever as the coming of God into our lives.

The apostle Paul had an encounter with Jesus on the Damascus road that forever changed his life. And throughout his writings he is trying to find the words to make sense of this momentous and transformative event. In the language of philosophy, the Jesus encounter affected a paradigm shift for Paul. In the language of psychology, this was a gestalt experience. In the language of religion, this was a numinal encounter.

Paul, of course, uses his own language. He speaks of it as the movement from death to life. One becomes a new creation in Christ. The old has fallen into the background. The new has taken center-stage. And this new life has brought us peace with God, forgiveness of sin, and the healing and empowering presence of the Spirit.

In the light of the above, it is worth asking why conversion, and the religious experience of so many in the Western World, in contrast, remains so shallow. It's as if the pawn and not the mighty queen is at work. While the answers to this question may be complex and varied, some things do stand out. In our supposed need for a therapeutic God we have emasculated God's transcendence. And in our narcissistic preoccupations, we have become afraid of God's rulership in our lives.

But God's presence and action are no mere pawns. The God of the universe is no mere religious play toy. And while God's power remains linked to his gentleness, there is nothing that God cannot do in his work of transformation and renewal.

Reflection: How can I become more open to God's power and grace in my life?

FAITH

THE HEART'S TRUE HOME

A THOUGHTFUL AND
PASSIONATE FAITH

*I pray that out of his glorious riches he may strengthen you with power
through his Spirit in your inner being so that Christ may dwell in your
hearts through faith.*

Ephesians 3:16-17a

William James once made the observation that religion "is either a dull habit or an acute fever." But while one or the other may be true of some individuals, and also of some religious traditions, there are more balanced perspectives that lie between these two polarizations.

The idea that one should always be fire hot in one's walk of faith, otherwise one is stone cold, is clearly experiential nonsense. And the main reason why this is so, is because the overwhelming testimony of the history of Christian spirituality, is that there are seasons and contours in the life of faith.

The spiritual journey is far more complex that being either hot or cold, passionate or dull, full of the Spirit or weighted down with the barnacles of tradition. Spirituality knows both the joy of ecstasy, and the pain of the dark night of the soul.

While balance is not what we should necessarily strive for in the walk of faith, since that may suggest flattening out the rich contours of religious experience, wholeness and integration should be part of the spiritual quest.

Some broad brush strokes on this canvass involve a corresponding emphasis on Word and Spirit, contemplation and action, worship and service, head and heart, and individual piety and communal nurture and care.

The history of Christianity is replete with one-sided emphases. Spiritual fervor, but lacking theological depth is exemplified in Montanism. A contemplation leading to a world-denying form of Christianity marred some aspects of monasticism. A pietism that led to sheer subjectivism has characterized some sections of evangelicalism. The list could go on.

But the rich texture of the biblical story invites us to embrace a redeemer who is also the creator. It celebrates a God who is Wholly Other and who is wholly concerned. It calls us to love God and the neighbor. It invites us to a theologically formed mind and a Spirit-shaped heart.

Faith need not be the one or the other, as in William James' paradigm. It can be faith shaped by understanding. And understanding lived in faith. It is knowledge lived in hope, and hope shaped by knowledge. It is prayer expressed in action, and action born out of prayer.

Reflection: In what part of my life do I need to move into greater wholeness and integration?

TRANSFORMATIONAL FAITH

"Have faith in God" Jesus answered. "I tell you the truth, if anyone says to the mountain, 'Go throw yourself into the sea' and does not doubt in his heart but believes that what he says will happen, it will be done for him.'"

Mark 11:22-23

There is nothing monochrome about the biblical notion of faith. Faith is a rich and textured concept pregnant with meaning that puts us in touch with God's renewing and transforming activity.

Faith is God's gift, and anything that comes from the hand of the living God is never sterile or merely repetitive. God's gifts are life-giving and empowering. And the gift of faith helps us to see who we truly are in God's presence. In God's light we see our creatureliness, our sinfulness, and our folly. But that is never all that we see. We also see God's provision in Christ, his grace, and the welcome of his embrace.

Faith is not only God's precious gift, but also our response. We thankfully grasp God's extended hand. We revel in his grace, and rejoice in his forgiveness and welcome. And throughout life's journey we continue to turn to the God who has called us. Thus faith becomes the very heartbeat of our spiritual existence.

This faith as a permanent, but renewable deposit in our lives, operates not only in the midst of the assembly of faith and in the place of worship—although there it can be strengthened and energized—but also in the quiet place, and in the times of the dark

31

night of the soul. Faith, therefore, knows its times of strength and power, but also its seasons of weakness and fragility.

But while the life of faith has its prosaic regularity, it also has its times of creativity and generativity. August Hermann Francke speaks of the faith that transforms us by the grace of God, and the power of the Spirit, so that a new style of life occurs that issues in "risk-taking faith" (*Glaubens-Wagnisse*). This is our faith-filled response to the call of God as we are drawn to prayer, and out into the world as servants of the Kingdom of God.

This kind of faith may lead us in the direction of a St. Francis or a Mother Teresa, a Dietrich Bonhoeffer or a Dorothy Day, an Oscar Romero or a Jacques Ellul. This type of risk-taking-faith through the love of God and for the sake of others, may draw us into creating new communities of care, apostolic zeal, the work for justice or the challenge of prophetic annunciation and denunciation.

This renewing and mobilizing faith may move us to the quiet places of prayer, to healing prayers for others, or to the ministry of exorcism. It is a faith that envisions the breaking in of the Kingdom of Heaven in the here and the now. It is a faith that stubbornly pronounces a no to the world's agenda, and a yes to God's grace and power.

Reflection: How may we move from a prosaic to a transformational faith?

32

WITNESS

For we are to God the aroma of Christ among those who are being saved and those who are perishing. To the one we are the smell of death; to the other, the fragrance of life. And who is equal to such a task?

2 Corinthians 2:15-16

Most of us are drawn to faith in Christ because of a recognition of our need for forgiveness, healing, renewal and empowerment. We have come to the point where we recognize that *our* ways don't work; that *our* reasons for being are inadequate; and that *our* own hopes for well-being and wholeness are on shaky ground. And so, due to the amazing persistence of the love of God towards us and the renewing work of the Spirit, we are drawn into the Gospel story and into the mystery of what Christ has done in giving us life through his death.

However, we soon come to the realization that our coming to faith is not simply about us and our well-being. Coming to faith in Christ is the welcome to be blessed, but also to bless others. Coming to faith in Christ is the invitation to newness of life, but also to point others in the same direction. Faith in Christ begins our journey towards wholeness, but also to serve others.

Thus, the first movement of the Christian life is being drawn into the mystery of faith. The second movement is beginning to participate in the work of the Kingdom of God. Both movements are intrinsic to what it means to be a Christian. And both movements are dynamically inter-related. Faith leads to service, and service energizes our faith. Receiving the grace of God empowers us to bless others, serving others draws us to drink anew of God's goodness and mercy.

The church in the Western World is weak in its understanding and praxis of this double movement. Infected by individualism and self-interest, Christians in the West see the Gospel more as a blessing for them, rather than as a call to serve God's reign in the world. Therefore, the church in the West needs to recover a vision of a life of witness. St. Francis of Assisi puts this well, "preach the Gospel at all times, if necessary, use words."

Thus it is in our family, in our neighborliness, in the way we work, in the way we run our businesses and corporations, in the way we create and conduct the multitude of institutions and organizations, and in all of our relationships, that we are to reflect the gospel—good news that speaks of peace with God, forgiveness towards others, the healing of relationships, and the doing of God's shalom in our world.

Witness to Christ is not the extra that I may choose to take on. It is intrinsic to who I am as a follower of Christ. Being blessed by his grace, I want to reflect that to others. And if Christ was willing to give his life for me, then I must be willing to wash the feet of the world.

Reflection: How can the life of Christ more fully impact me so that I may serve others?

THE BLESSINGS OF REVERSAL

I will give you the treasures of darkness, riches stored in secret places, so that you may know that I am the Lord, the God of Israel, who summons you by name.

Isaiah 45:3

We live in a world which continues to eulogize our status, success, and achievements. Our productivity is celebrated, and little is made of the value of the inner life. Yet in the final analysis our externalization is premised on contemplation. While this is not to suggest that we nurture the inner life only in order to be effective and productive, there is nevertheless an intimate connection between what we do and what we are.

That we need to grow in the inner life is a pressing issue given the spiritual superficiality of much of the Western church. It is all the more pressing in that some Christian groups make the development of the inner life simply the growth from immaturity to maturity.

But the contours of the growth of the inner life are much more complex than this simplistic evolutionary upward movement. It therefore comes as no surprise when the Church father, Basil of Caesarea, suggests that the movement of the spiritual life is not so much "from darkness to light, but from light to divine darkness."

This in no way suggests that we do not move in initial conversion and faith from the darkness of our alienation, waywardness, and sin, into the light of God's mercy, grace, and embrace. Rather, Basil suggests that once we have come into the light of God's revelation and renewal, there is the possibility that we may move into the darkness of the mystery of the God who is still with us.

Divine darkness is not the fruit of our alienation and sin, but is the way of God with us, moving us from the certainties of faith into its mystery and awe. Unfortunately, so often the certainty of our certainties does not nourish the life of faith, but diminishes it. Even in our Christian walk, we can so easily become self-confident and self-dependent. Little wonder, therefore, that we need to enter into God's mysterious way with us.

If God's way with us includes the journey of divine darkness, then God invites us to move from revelation to mystery, from certainty to hope, from answers to deeper questions, from knowing to faith, and from security into radical vulnerability. This is no easy way for us, and we may well question whether God has abandoned us. Moreover, we may well have to move from the certainty of our ready answers into the deep silence of trust and faith.

At the most fundamental level, we are recognizing that God's way with and in us, is shrouded in the mystery of his love. Thus while we may be able to confess the certainty of God's presence in the seeming absence, we may have to acknowledge that we do not fully understand God's way with us.

Yet, this in no way needs to undermine our confession that God is greater than what we do not understand, and greater than our uncertainties.

Reflection: In what ways have you experienced God's surprising reversals and mysterious workings?

CURIOSITY BEGINS

Now we know that if the earthly tent we live in is destroyed, we have a building from God, an eternal house in heaven, not built by human hands. Meanwhile we groan longing to be clothed with our heavenly dwelling.

2 Corinthians 5:1-2

The church father Tertullian once made the statement, "all curiosity ceases after the Gospel." While we may agree with what he basically means, namely, that having found Christ in the gospels our restless hearts have come home, we should nevertheless disagree. In fact, his statement should be completely turned around. All curiosity *begins* with the gospel.

I am referring to a whole new kind of curiosity. For having satisfied the curiosity that comes out of our lostness and alienation and having found new life in Christ through the Spirit, our searching hearts do not come to rest. In fact, they are activated. And we begin to live out of a curiosity spawned by faith.

This new curiosity has multiple contours. It is not simply a curiosity about spiritual things. Rather, it is a curiosity that embraces all of life and the life to come. Thus this curiosity draws us to know more fully the biblical story. It also invites us to understand the life of the people of God in the church's long march in history. But more comprehensively, it engages us to begin to see all of life from the perspective of the gospel. This includes the life of prayer as much as that of politics.

The heart of this new curiosity, however, has to do with seeking to know the heart and mind of God. It is seeking to know the wisdom and the ways of God. Thus this curiosity is not simply to gain lots of information about the Bible and the church. Its central motif lies elsewhere. It is a curiosity that probes the secrets of the Kingdom of God.

In saying this, I am in no way implying that this curiosity is the quest for the esoteric. I do not have a knowledge for a special elite in view. Nor am I in any way referring to claims made by some regarding the end of the world as we know it and the return of Christ. I have something quite different in view.

The secrets of the Kingdom of God enunciated in Scripture and sculpted on the pages of history, have to do with the mystery of God's providential care for a world that is persistently in flight from the embrace of God. The heart of this secret is the power of the cross of Christ in reversing the gasps of death into the birth pangs of new life. These secrets have to do with the persistence of the church, despite failure and weakness, and the mysterious work of the Spirit in the church and the world bringing renewal and hope.

True curiosity begins with the gospel. For having come to new life in God, we begin to gaze upon our world with new love and a different hope. We are amazed at what God has done. And we wonder what will yet take place. Since we ourselves do not make the end of history, we live towards the unveiling of God's final future.

The basic stance of the Christian before God, in the church, and in the world, is not one of narrow certainties, but one of boundless curiosity and awe. This is the nature of faith seeking understanding.

Reflection: In what ways do awe and curiosity need to be restored in my life?

INNER FRAGILITY

Why are you downcast, O my soul? Why so disturbed within me? Put your hope in God, for I will yet praise him, my Savior and my God.

Psalm 42:5

The Christian life can only be lived with courage, hope, and realism. While most would agree that it is lived in hope, which along with love and faith is one of the Christian virtues, the reference to other terms may be surprising to some. However, I think that they are fundamental to the way we are called to live.

Let me explain: It doesn't take courage to live the Christian life when such a life is cast in escapist or idealist terms. If we hold that God will always keep us safe in a big bad world or that only good will come our way because we are the people of God, then we are hardly called to live with courage.

But this idealism is not rooted in the biblical story, nor in the church's long testimony over two thousand years. As Christians we do not magically transcend the pain and brokenness of our world. We are not excluded from natural disasters, sickness, the difficulties of life, the injustice of our world and the inevitability of death.

This of course is not to suggest that we experience and process these things in the same way as others. We need and should not. While others may see these things as the movement of fate which they may curse, we may see these things as the signs of the falleness of our world, and the signals to turn to God in repentance and faith.

What this suggests is that realism is to be a part of our perspective as much as that of hope. There is little point in making out that life is nicer than it is. Put differently, Christians of all people should know how to face the brokenness of our world and of our own lives. For at the heart of the biblical story is a God, who not only enters our pain, but takes that pain upon himself offering us life and freedom.

As a result, Soren Kierkegaard's comment that "there is not one single living human being who does not despair a little, who does not secretly harbor an unrest, an inner strife" should not be applied only to the person who has not yet come to faith. It is also true of the person of faith. We are troubled, often afraid, sometimes fearful, and live with doubts. We struggle with family, relational, identity and work issues. We are affected by and contribute to the psycho-pathology of our society and culture.

There is little point of living the Christian life on the basis of denying the state of our world and of our own lives. Thus the contemplative experience is not only the impulse towards the heavenly, but also one of discerning the earthly. But this discernment of the earthly can only be done well in the light of the faith and hope that God's Kingdom is amongst us, and his grace is freely given.

The troubles within and without need not be the seedbed of despair, but the incentive for prayer. They are the traces and reminders of our need to flee to the God who is a present help in times of trouble.

Reflection: How can I face troubles within and without in the light of God's grace?

TRUST
EXPERIENCING GOODNESS

THE SMILE OF GOD

He makes grass grow for the cattle, and plants for man to cultivate—
bringing forth food from the earth: wine that gladdens the heart of
man, oil to make his face shine and bread that sustains his heart.

Psalm 104:14-15

It all depends on what is in our hearts that causes us to see things differently. Some see nothing, because they bring empty and dead hearts to their seeing. Others see nothing but difficulty and dread in our social landscape, because they draw from the wells of fear. Others see only negativity, because their hearts are embalmed in a critical spirit.

While all of these are inadequate ways of seeing, this is not to suggest that we should see life through rose colored glasses, and through the illusion of idealism. In the final analysis, that is a form of escapism.

What then may we see? And what it is that should reverberate in our hearts? Morris West provides some answers to the first question. He writes, "there is a stamp of love upon the world, however much of it is defaced by hatred and violence." This double perspective regarding the world's beauty as well as its pain, reflects the march of God's grace and the stubborn persistence of evil. It also reflects the divided nature of our hearts torn between faith, hope and love, and the bitter realism spawned by sin's pervasive presence.

It should hardly surprise us that we find it difficult to live this kind of dialectic, and therefore, we tend to move to one or other end of these two poles. It is understandable that we may wish to drop the evil part of the polarity and end up with an optimistic humanism. It is also possible that we drop the vision of faith and see only a world marred by our inhumanity to one another.

To see the stamp of love on our world need not be the visionary madness of the spiritual sage. Nature is charged with a God-inspired grandeur. And in the human community we also see the continuity of institutions that serve the common good. And there are people who weave the texture of care and sharing in their relationships. Not only is the world not abandoned by God, but God's grace permeates the human community, and his Spirit hovers pregnantly over all that is good.

Yet evil, nevertheless, continues its pompous march. Embedded in the structures of injustice and oppression, and ever playing in all of our hearts the songs of fear, hatred, selfishness and rebellion, evil is as much a part of our world as is the finger of God.

In seeing both, we are not invited to live an impossible dualism, but to live in faith and hope that God's grace will be the final trumpet call. Its music invites us to the banquet of the Kingdom of Heaven.

Reflection: Where has this double movement of grace and the reality of evil left your heart and your vision?

GOD IN THE SHADOWS

Hear my prayer, O Lord; let my cry for help come to you. Do not hide your face from me when I am in distress. Turn your ear to me; when I call, answer me quickly.

Psalm 102:1-2

Our Western propensity is to over-categorize and to over-polarize. Things are either black or white, false or true. In the Asian context things are different. There things are more both/and. But in the realm of personal relationships things become infinitely complex and frequently ambiguous.

This is also true in our often fragile relationship with God. God is both the sovereign Lord of the universe, and the vulnerable babe in Bethlehem. And in his relationship with us, God is both lovingly invasive and strangely silent. And while we speak of God's covenant faithfulness with us, this does not mean that God's way with us is nicely predictable.

St. Anthony having gone through an incredibly difficult time asked God: "Where were you, Lord, during this time?" He received this answer, "nearer than ever to thee." This somewhat surprising answer hints at the complexity of our relationship with God. It is never simply a matter of presence or absence. We also experience God in the shadows.

Many of the difficulties that we experience in our relationship with God have to do with the faulty and unrealistic expectations that we have regarding who God is, and the way he works in human affairs. Not only do we forget that God is the mystery of

45

the Trinity and cannot be reduced to a manageable Christology, but we also forget that God has made his way known in surprising acts and pregnant stories, rather than in clear explanations and propositions.

As a result of the impact of the Enlightenment, we have dragged too many rational categories to the biblical story. And as the impact of technology ever more fully pervades our thinking and acting, we have dragged too many schemes and paradigms into our understanding of spirituality.

While I in no way wish to minimize that we need to love God with our minds, we nevertheless need to bow before the mystery of God's transcendence. God works in mysterious ways his wonders to perform. And God is with us in ways beyond our immediate understanding.

God sustains us in ways that we cannot even begin to comprehend. His ways of intervention are surprising. God's blessings come ever so unexpectedly. The movements of his Spirit are ever renewing.

So often, it is after the difficulties and the crises that we see the shadow of God's presence. God was there, but did not take center stage. He spoke, but there was no bellowing voices. He gave, but we did not readily discern his gifts.

Reflection: In what way can I begin to discern more carefully God's presence with me and in our world?

GOD'S REVELATION

After this, the word of the Lord came to Abram in a vision: "Do not be afraid, Abram. I am your shield, your very great reward."

Genesis 15:1

One of the things that we must never forget is that the Bible is full of accounts of God appearing to people. Whether that be Abram, Moses or Isaiah, the central motif is the same: God wishes to make himself known, and he has important and life changing things to say to us.

It is both sad and ironic that the contemporary Christian church has largely fallen silent about the appearance of God. The church has almost given the impression that God no longer does this. Indirectly, the church seems to say that God is now bound to the pages of the Bible and secondarily to our church, our confessions, and liturgies. Thus once God appeared in person. Now God appears through indirect means, and the church is the conveyor of those means.

I see lots of problems with this kind of construction. It gives the church far too much power. But of greater concern is that it places the personalness of God in the past. Those ancient days were the days of an encounter with the divine and were days of the miraculous. These days we are more rational.

But what this may mean is not that God has changed, but that we have succumbed to the values of our contemporary culture. In other words, our scientific and rationalistic approach to life has infected our way of relating to God. Mystery has been replaced by explanation, and mysticism by rationalism.

St. Anselm once prayed: "I will never find you unless you show yourself to me." This prayer needs to be recaptured by the contemporary church. Its central confidence is that God does and will reveal himself. This does not mean that God will not use Scripture or the sacraments of the church. But it means that we may not and should not set limits.

Moreover, one can know Scripture and participate in the sacraments and not know God in the sense that one has had an encounter with the living God. And at heart, this is the essence of the Christian faith. It is being known by and knowing God, and this knowing while intellectual, is fundamentally a matter of faith and of the heart.

And the "certainty" of that lies not simply in religious rituals, but in *encounter*. God reveals. God draws near. God breaks into our consciousness.

If we cannot recapture the mystery of faith and the presence of God in our lives, we will finally become spiritual orphans who lose our way. A rational faith cannot resist the rationalization of life and of our world. Only a faith that is sustained by God's Spirit is a living and enduring faith.

Reflection: How can we open ourselves more fully to the mystery of faith?

HUMILITY

And being found in appearance as a man he humbled himself and became obedient to death—even death on a cross!

Philippians 2:8

Our modern age doesn't think much of the virtue of humility. In fact, it doesn't regard humility as a virtue but more as a problem. The reasons for this turn around are many and complex. But the basics are clear. Our culture regards self-assertion and self-preoccupation as virtues, and humility is seen as some sort of self-negation.

One area where the idea of humility has been particularly difficult is in the domestic realm. Humility on the part of the wife, or the female partner, for example, has been linked to notions of docility and subservience. Little wonder when humility is so misunderstood and misused that a reaction to the whole concept sets in. Here humility is closer to the idea to "humiliate."

It is necessary, therefore, for us to rehabilitate this word. While in the ancient world "humility" had the meaning of "lowly" and was used in a negative sense, in the biblical tradition it was held to be an important aspect of true spirituality.

Throughout the pages of the Old Testament the humble were those who lived a life of dependence on God. God the Creator and Liberator and great Carer of his people was seen as the giver of life and all good things. Life was, therefore, to be lived in relation to, in dependence upon, and in gratitude towards this life sustaining God. And those who lived in this way were called the humble.

49

In the pages of the New Testament, Jesus is seen as God's humble servant. Andrew Murray puts it simply: "because Christ had thus humbled himself before God, and God was ever before him, he found it possible to humble himself before men [and women] too, and to be the servant of all."

This example we are called to follow. We too are to acknowledge God as the source of life. And God is the one we seek to obey. Out of this relationship with God we are empowered to serve others. And in this we wear the mantle of humility.

Humility is not self-abasement. It is a posture of openness to the God of all grace, and being willing to receive from God. Humility positions us before God in a way that our willful independence does not.

Throughout the long history of Christian spirituality humility was held to be the mother of all virtues. This is understandable. For while pride and self-sufficiency cut us off from the sources of renewal and sustenance, humility becomes the bowl of receptivity.

The humble, those who wholly look to their God, are the ones who are blessed and will be the peacemakers in our world. Those who lack this grace may well become the warmongers of our world.

Reflection: What kind of self-identity is the outcome of being graced by humility?

WEAVING TRUST

Trust in the Lord with all your heart and lean not on your own understanding; in all your ways acknowledge him and he will make your paths straight.

Proverbs 3:5-6

Trust is the innate gift of childhood. How readily children entrust themselves to parents, teachers and even strangers. How willing they are to believe, accept and receive.

This trust is also centered in a God they cannot see, and who they do not understand. But they believe God's goodness and his power. Children, therefore, can pray with a touching simplicity and directness that moves the heart of God.

I can remember my nine year old praying that Daddy would get better, now. Within that same day, that innocent prayer was answered.

But this gentle texture of trust is readily broken on the rocky journey of life. Parents fail us. Teachers are not always fair or right. Friends can be cruel. And God does not always answer our prayers in the way we expect.

Moreover, we are soon taught not to trust, but to question everything we read and see. And while critical thinking is a necessary part of adult identity, the icy fingers of skepticism so easily encircle our hoping hearts. And in an age where we have become the center of our world, where our prowess is lauded, and where our scientific endeavors can save us, trust in God is soon seen as infantile and superstitious.

Yet surprisingly, trust does persist. It is a more hardy plant than we had first realized. There is so much that we simply have to accept. A lifetime is insufficient to question everything. And the very fabric of our social existence involves trust.

So, several matters press upon us. The first, is to make the move from an unthinking childhood trust to a thought-through position. Secondly, it's imperative to realize that the real issue is not, no trust at all, but what do I trust in. Do I trust simply in myself or do I also trust God and others? Do I trust simply in human achievement or do I also trust in the grace of God.

Teilhard de Chardin reminds us to "trust in the slow work of God." He means, that God works according to his own careful purposes. But to sharpen that we may say that trust *is* the slow work of God. As we move from a childhood trust to an adult one, trust is to be rewoven. Broken trust can be mended. Doubting trust can be filled with hope. Trust is God's slow restorative work in us.

Trust for the long and precarious journey of life, can finally only be sustained by faith in the trustworthy One—the God who has reached out to us in redeeming love, and who promises to be with us in sickness and health, in our living and our dying.

Reflection: Where do the delicate membranes of trust need to be mended in my life?

HOPE

LIVING IN ANTICIPATION

WITH OPEN HANDS

*Why are you downcast, O my soul? Why so disturbed within me? Put
your hope in God, for I will yet praise him, my Savior and my God.*

Psalm 42:11

We can see it so clearly in the poor. With time one's social and
economic difficulties become the inward reality of one's
life. Powerlessness and hopelessness sculpt one's inner psyche. We
call this the internalization of a culture of poverty. And with its all
pervasive presence a fatalism starves the membranes of one's being
of the oxygen of hope.

This disempowering scenario is not restricted to the poor. We
all have parts of our life where the doors and windows have been
closed, and where we have shut down the possibility of change and
renewal. In these empty and barren spaces of our life, we dare not
hope for anything better. Better, we say, the pain of not having,
than the pain of disappointed hopes.

Bernard Malamud expressed this sentiment through one of his
characters: "if you've had nothing, you're afraid of too much." And
to elaborate further, if we have closed down on the possibility of
any change, then we are lost in the wasteland of our fears.

It is therefore important that we ask, how may others help us
to move beyond this negativity? Do they help by giving what is
lacking? Do they pray for the restoration of hope? Do they cast
out the spirits of fear and resignation? Do they work for the greater
general good in our community so that a greater justice may
prevail that will benefit all?

Maybe all, or some, or none of these suggestions will move us in new directions. But people are usually much too quick with their advice and helping strategies. The recovery of hope, and an openness to new possibilities, come so often more as the surprise than through the well-intentioned efforts of others.

The seeds of hope may spring up in variety of ways. One source of the birth of hope is the willingness to revisit the desolate places of our life, but to do so in the presence of the One who bends towards us with wounded hands. We turn to the One who comes riding not on a victory horse, but on a donkey of shame and rejection.

It is never loss or not-having which in and of itself disempowers us. It is rather that with our loss we feel that we have been abandoned and forgotten. We are lost to others, and thus become lost to ourselves. Thus the recovery of hope lies not so much in receiving hoped for solutions, but in the embrace of the God who suffers for and with us.

Hope is the fruit of the resurrection which reminds us that in God's scheme of things death does not have the last word. So we are invited to stretch out our limp hands, heavy heart, and fearful disposition towards the God who joins us in our sorrow, and invites us to pilgrimage. This forward movement calls us to open our doors, and our hands, so that God can give us the buds of new life.

Reflection: Where are the places in my life that need to be opened to the renewing work of God's Spirit?

THOSE DANCING FEET

You turned my wailing into dancing; you removed my sackcloth and clothed me with joy, that my heart may sing to you and not be silent. O Lord my God, I will give you thanks forever.

Psalm 30:11-12

Joy is nothing other than pure gift. And it comes to us at unexpected times. It may well up within us in the dreary and desolate places of our lives. It may also erupt with the sweet breath of God upon us, the sudden visit of a friend, the melody of a familiar song, the vivid reds of a sunset, the majestic wing of an eagle in full flight.

Joy takes us beyond the dullness of our everyday routines. It is one of the whispers from the edge of eternity. It is God's reminder that his beneficence is towards us. Roberta Bondi is therefore correct, that "God draws us to joy."

While we may want to say that we find joy in the simplest experiences of life, it is more correct to recognize *that joy finds us* in the gurgles of a baby, the whispers of a lover, and in the midst of a boisterous song. It visits us in the completion of a job well done, the wisdom of a friend, and in the welcome of an unexpected guest.

But while joy may open its song to us in the many and varied moments and movements of our life, it most enticingly wings its way to our inner being borne by the life-giving Spirit. Joy is God's gift, and is most fully experienced in God's presence.

In every aspect of life we may experience God's presence. Service, rest, work, friendship and celebration are some of the many settings where joy may visit us. But we may especially experience the gift of joy in communal worship, and in the place of private solitude.

In worship in the community of faith we join with our brothers and sisters, and with the church of all ages and all places, to remember and celebrate the faithfulness of the God who journeys with his people. Here we recognize that we are a part of a much greater whole. Here we celebrate that we are in solidarity with others who will help bear the load. Here we are grateful that we are not alone. And here we sing the songs of faith, hope and longing for the power of the resurrection to carry us into the fullness of the age to come.

But it is also in the quiet place that joy may visit us. As we lay our concerns at God's feet, and place our life in God's hand, and as we remember the way in which God loves us, joy reminds us that the pain and struggle of life do not have the last word.

It would be wonderful to say that we are made for joy. But it is more correct to say that we are made for life lived in God's presence. We do not know all that life will bring us, but it will have its share of difficulty and disappointments. It can also have its moments of deep joy, as we celebrate the power of the resurrection of Christ, who breaks the chains that oppress and sets captives free.

Reflection: Where are the places in my life where I may dance for joy?

A DISCERNING HOPE

O Israel, put your hope in the Lord, for with the Lord is unfailing love and with him is full redemption.

Psalm 130:7

Hope, that human quality that looks to the future and the goodness that will come, is easily misplaced and is always open to manipulation and distortion.

Our contemporary culture offers much. Almost anything is available. Almost everything is possible. And we are invited to pursue the illusory dream of success and prosperity.

While one may hope in anything and hope for everything, biblical hope has a quality all of its own. It has a center that needs to be carefully discerned and lovingly embraced. And so the words of Georges Bernanos are helpful: "in order to be prepared to hope in what does not deceive, we must first lose hope in everything that does deceive."

Many of our hopes need to be converted and transformed, for what we hope for is not central to the biblical vision of a life of faith. And not only does society offer us misplaced hopes, the church in its teaching and preaching ministry may also offer us hopes that lack a good foundation.

The center of hope in Scripture is God himself in his love, grace, and generosity. And the movement of hope in the biblical story, is to continue to hope in God when we are so sorely tempted to look elsewhere because of other voices or we are disappointed in God's way with us.

Christian spirituality of hope is a discerning hope. It has the eyes to see false promises because it is characterized by a trust that believes that God's ways are the ways of life.

This hope needs to be sustained because God's way with us is as much shrouded in mystery as it is revealed in the clarity of love.

The Christian hope is that God's Kingdom will continue to impact our lives and our world. That God's beneficent face is towards us. That goodness will continue to erupt. That evil will finally not prevail. And that the promise of the resurrection, and of new heavens and new earth, are rooted in Christ's victory over sin and death.

Our hope should not be in the church, but in the God who continues to renew the church. Our hope should not lie in our own faith, but in the God who continues to uphold us.

Sadly so often, we only turn in hope to God when all our other hopes have been decimated. May we instead live in hope and faith in God because he alone is the way of life and truth.

Reflection: What false hopes need to be identified and discarded?

THE WOUND OF HOPE

Why are you downcast, O my soul? Why so disturbed within me? Put your hope in God, for I will yet praise him, my Savior and my God.
Psalm 42:5

The Christian mystic, Julian of Norwich, speaks of the three wounds that are to mark the Christian: "the wound of contrition" (for sin); "the wound of compassion" (for others); and "the wound of longing" (for God).

It is rather obvious that the first two should spring out of the latter. It is out of our orientation towards God, and our longing for God, that everything else springs. And that longing is spurred on by the love that God has shown towards us.

What is not so obvious is the language of wounding. In spirituality we use the language of healing not that of wounding. And we doubt whether anything good can come from wounds. Wounds are associated with pain and distress.

But as Christians we *are* marked people. The death and resurrection of Christ has impacted and marked us, and baptism is a sign of this.

Marked by the grace of Christ, and carried and nurtured by the Holy Spirit, there is within us a profound and deep longing. We long for God. We long for the Kingdom of God to come more fully amongst us. We long for an empowered church. We long for a world of peace and justice. We long for new heavens and a new earth.

And at times this longing becomes an almost unbearable ache. This longing is like a wound we carry within us.

This is essential to a life lived in hope. We live in expectation. We long for what is yet to come, for what may yet be given.

This wound of longing needs to be carefully safeguarded and nurtured. We can so easily become enamored with what is around us, and satisfied with what we have. Or more specifically, we can begin to doubt that things can change. Or more seriously, we can doubt God's providential and beneficent care. We may begin to think that longing for God is like longing to grasp the wind.

Longing for God is a rightful recognition of who God is and who we are. It is a sign of reconciliation and friendship. But more importantly, it is the center of the quest for deeper union with God. It is the recognition that a life lived in and for God is life that achieves its greatest purpose.

While this mysticism is not understood by our pragmatic age, it is understood by the language of the seeking heart.

Reflection: *In what ways do I long for God?*

LIVING IN HOPE

Hope deferred makes the heart sick, but a longing fulfilled is a tree of life.

Proverbs 13:12

There are people who have given up on discovering and experiencing a meaningful life. Life is seen as difficult and unfair.

Others are deeply disappointed with life and this means that they are disappointed with others, or with themselves, or with God. For others, the words of novelist Bryce Courtenay may come closer to the mark: "when you cut hope from the heart the hole you leave is filled with the worms of hate."

To live life well, one lives in hope. This suggests the fundamental future orientation of the human being. Life bends itself towards the future and anticipates what that future may be like.

It is important to reflect on how we live in this anticipatory way. For some, the anticipation is primarily passive. Life happens to them. The future will come and bring with it its blessings and difficulties.

But for others the future is managed and manipulated. They work and plan for the future. They attempt as much as possible to make things happen. The future is largely their design, at least this is what they wish.

Between resignation and control lie other options. And the Christian approach to life is one of these in-between options.

The future is not ours. It is God's. But God has called us to freedom. In freedom we can hope, pray and work in relation to what lies in front of us. Freedom also opens us to the surprises that may come our way.

This freedom is textured in a particular way. It is not a freedom that is marked by lack of responsibility. It is not a freedom simply for ourselves.

Our freedom in relation to the future is a freedom in God for his purposes to mend all of creation. Thus it is a freedom in which we seek the will of God and his glory. And it is a freedom for the blessing of others.

A heart full of hope is also a heart of love. And a heart of love is thankful for the past, perseveres in the present and anticipates the future as a gift from the heart and hand of the Beloved.

Hope carries us into the future overcoming the shoals of doubt and pessimism. As such hope is the elixir of life.

Reflection: How do I live towards the future?

COMMUNITY

SHARING LIFE TOGETHER

COMMUNITY IN AND
THROUGH CHRIST

*The body is a unit, though it is made up of many parts; and though
all its parts are many, they form one body. So it is with Christ. For
we were all baptized by one Spirit into one body—whether Jews or
Greeks, slave or free—and we were all given the one Spirit to drink.*
1 Corinthians 12:12-13

Community is not unique to Christians. Humans form various
forms of association, some of which resemble communities.
Various religions also form particular communities, and
monasticism, for example, is not unique to Roman Catholicism.
There are also Buddhist monastic communities.

But Christian community formed in and through Christ has
some particular characteristics. Stanley Hauerwas gives us a hint
of what that may look like. He notes, "Christian community . . .
is not primarily about togetherness. It is about the way of Jesus
Christ with those whom Christ calls to himself."

Allow me to spell out more fully what that may look like.

The heart of Christian community is not, first of all, particular
structures and models of association. The heart of the matter lies
elsewhere. It has to do with people embracing the love, forgiveness
and renewal that Christ offers. And joining in the challenge to
outwork the gospel of Christ in all areas of life, including the way
we come together for worship, teaching, sacraments, fellowship
and service.

Christian community thus has its beginning in the renewing and transformative work of Christ, a work that motivates us to love and serve our brothers and sisters in Christ, and the neighbor, even our enemies. And this community is sustained by nothing less than the presence of Christ.

However, Christ does not get us started, and then we do the rest by ourselves. If that occurs, then community will soon devolve into a social club. For Christian community to be sustained, we continue to need the presence and power of Christ with us and in us.

When community is empowered by Christ through the Spirit then certain things will continue to be present. There will be the joy of association, whatever forms that association may take. Together with Christ, and each other, becomes one of the ways of encouragement and empowerment.

Moreover, it will be a community of openness and hospitality. A community enclosed in upon itself has shut out both Christ and the neighbor. A community living in Christ is a community with its arms open to the world.

Such a community is fundamentally a community of forgiveness. Here moralism and legalism do not reign supreme, but love, generosity and forgiveness do.

Finally, such a community lives with a sense of self-forgetfulness. It is not fully aware of how it has been gifted and blessed by God. Thus it can live, with a childlike innocence and joy, the values of the Kingdom of Christ.

Reflection: How can my present religious association become more like a Christian community?

THE COMMUNITY OF FAITH

May the God who gives endurance and encouragement give you a spirit of unity among yourselves as you follow Christ Jesus, so that with one heart and mouth you may glorify the God and Father of our Lord Jesus Christ.

Romans 15:5-6

One of the urgent matters of our time is for the church to reinvent and to reformulate itself. This is not a call for a radical discontinuity. I am not in anyway proposing that the church should sever itself from the riches of its two thousand year history and tradition. Such a move would be a form of suicide. It is also a form of gross arrogance. What makes us think that we now have all the answers for the church's life, worship, teaching and service?

But reformulation is appropriate, if we mean by that a discerning reappropriation of the blessings of the past and the lessons of yesteryear. This, of course, must be done in the light of the New Testament vision of the church, and in response to contemporary challenges and issues. What is playing itself out in this formulation is the recognition, that the way the church has structured its life together a hundred or fifty years ago, may not provide the most relevant way in which it can be church today.

The church of the cathedrals reflected a Christianity that shaped the dominant ethos and values of the society just as surely as its church spires dominated the horizon. The church today, as a minority movement in a predominantly secular world, is much more accurately depicted by the image of the house church, rather than by the cathedrals of yesteryear.

But whether cathedral or house church, the church's fundamental nature does not lie in its external and organizational structures. It lies rather in its internal life rooted in Christ, and expressed in relationships of solidarity and care.

Jürgen Moltmann in seeking to understand the heart of Christian community speaks of church as "Messianic fellowship," a "free society of equals" and a community of "open friendship."

Moltmann is right in emphasizing the importance of relationships at the heart of Christian community. But such relationships are not simply the fruit of psychological group dynamics. They are rooted in participating in the life that God gives. They come from a Christo-mysticism, where by the Spirit, we enter into the life of Christ by faith and obedience.

Thus Christian community is formed by the grace of God, and is sustained by the work of the Spirit. This means that the church will ever be renewed, as surely as it is sustained. The Spirit's work brings the new breath of God and refreshing waters to our tired souls, but can also bring renewal to our equally tired structures.

Reflection: How can we place ourselves open to the renewing work of the Spirit so that our communities of faith are not the product of mere sociological reconstruction, but of renewal of our life with God?

THE ACTS FOR TODAY

All the believers were together and had everything in common. Selling their possessions and goods, they gave to anyone as he had need.

Acts 2:44-45

The pages of the New Testament are full of the dangerous memories of early Christianity. These memories forged in the heat of the resurrected Messiah, and the outpouring of the Holy Spirit, and in the hope of the full arrival of God's Kingdom, empowered the early Christians to live radical lives.

One of the ways in which their vision of the Kingdom of God was outworked was in the form of radical Christian community. *Koinonia*—fellowship—meant a full participation in each other's lives, even to the point of economic sharing.

That this vision was not a temporary peculiarity of the early Jerusalem church is evidenced by the persistence of this vision. The late first century or early second century document, *The Didache*, notes "for if you have what is eternal in common, how much more should you have what is transient."

This vision at the heart of early Christian praxis has obvious implications for us today, as we seek to live our Christian lives in a world so fragmented, and in churches so characterized by institutional realities.

In many ways, Christians in the First World, are thrice orphans. We have lost a deep sense of spirituality which was meant to bring us into the embrace of God. Our families have become fragmented, and our social landscape alienating due to our individualism and loss of the common good. And even in our churches, we have become ecclesiastical orphans.

The church, for many, is the place where we access religious resources and services. And we do so with a consumer mentality. Church is hardly our spiritual home. There is frequently little sense of belonging and solidarity. We are more often strangers in Christ, rather than brothers and sisters in Christ. And while we may share the Word of God together and pray together, we don't share our homes, our lives, our dreams, and our resources.

The way of the enemy of our souls is to sow discord and to fragment community. The way of the world is to build pseudo-community, community that is not centered in the ways of God but in our own pretentions and human autonomy. The way of God builds a people. The way of Christ breaks down the barriers and brings about reconciliation. The way of the Spirit makes us one.

The way of our modern world has destroyed primary community. The way of our contemporary values has promoted the myth of an autonomous self. And the way of the present day church welcomes us to religious services, but not to community in Christ, involving the sharing of our lives in God's love. How impoverished we are, and how much we need to recapture the dangerous memories of early Christianity!

Reflection: How can I enter more fully into God's gift of community?

MOVEMENTS OF
THE SPIRITUAL LIFE

*Be imitators of God, therefore, as dearly loved children and live a life
of love, just as Christ loved us and gave himself up for us as a fragrant
offering and sacrifice to God.*

Ephesians 5:1-2

Some want to see the Christian life as one of arrival. After all, by
faith in Christ we have come home to the heart of God. Thus
justification by faith formalizes the miracle of reconciliation and
homecoming.

But while this image of arrival is powerful for understanding the
Christian life, a more comprehensive metaphor is that of journey.
One may speak of the movements of the spiritual life.

While the ancient writers on Christian spirituality thought of
movement in upward terms, particularly in the form of the ladder
that reached ever upwards towards God and Christian perfection,
there are other ways of understanding the Christian life.

The most fundamental, is movement involved in a dynamic
of relationship. God reaches out towards us in love and covenant
faithfulness, and empowers us with his life through the work of
the Holy Spirit. We respond to receive that life in faith, and seek to
orient our life to God's ways in love, obedience and service.

Healthy relationships are those of movement and growth. They
involve a deepening faithfulness and intimacy, as well as times of

struggle, difficulty and apathy. There is nothing static about the life of faith, and our walk with God.

Based on this dynamic, it is possible to discern some further contours. Henri Nouwen speaks of the movement flowing from the Eucharist as the movement from "communion to community to ministry."

This formulation may be seen a series of interlocking circles. Or formulated more dynamically as a hermeneutic circle, where each impacts the other, and is impacted itself by the effect it creates.

Thus the Eucharist both calls us to create Christian solidarity and community, and that very community in turn expresses something of the richness of the Lord's Supper. Or to put that differently, the gathering around bread and wine as a spiritual reality, calls us to the sociological reality of the community in Christ expressing a life together that gives meaning to the sacrament of Holy Communion.

Similarly, Christian community actualizes and authenticates itself in a life of service both within and outside of the community. And these acts of pastoral care, witness, and the work for justice, in turn call us back to the banqueting table for God's nourishment and sustenance.

The one element, whether that be communion, community or ministry makes little sense without the other. Each interpenetrates the other, making life a mosaic whole to the glory of God.

Reflection: Are there elements of this mosaic that need adjustment or recovery in my journey of faith?

A SACRAMENT TO THE WORLD

In the same way, let your light shine before men, that they may see your good deeds and praise your Father in heaven.

Matthew 5:16

Word and deed belong together. When we say we care, then acts of care must accompany our words. A word expressed in action makes a word authentic and powerful. Words stripped of the company of deeds soon become hollow. On the other hand, deeds need the word. The word gives meaning to the deed.

God's engagement with the world has always been the coming together of word and deed. God spoke and acted. God promised and brought deliverance. And in Jesus, God's word becomes flesh and blood.

In the mission of Jesus we see the proclamation of words of hope, and the acts and deeds of power. We hear the teaching on forgiveness, and the act of forgiving those who crucified him. We hear the mystery of a great love, and the practice of a love that serves and lays down its life. We hear the promise of the Kingdom for the poor, and the welcome of the poor to God's banqueting table. We may say that Jesus did not simply proclaim the word of God, but embodied that word. Thus he is the Living Word!

The challenge facing the contemporary community of faith is to live that same ethic. That Christians in the past were empowered to do this is writ large in the annals of church history, and particularly in the story of the Early Christianity. Christians expected to be martyrs. Like Jesus, they gave their lives in confessing and living of their faith.

Except in the Third World, we in the First World know little of such faith and commitment. Ours has become an easy consumer Christianity, where faith is basically for our self-development, and the church exists only to nourish us. We know little of commitment, service, and living to bless others.

And yet, that is precisely where part of the challenge lies. Lesslie Newbigin reminds us that the strategy of Jesus was not to write a book, or leave behind a body of teaching, but "to prepare a community … to be the bearer of the secret of the kingdom."

The community of faith as bearer of the kingdom is fundamentally a community of love, reconciliation, forgiveness, welcome, and service. Here the worship of God is central, and the desire to obey God is paramount. Here members serve and care for each other, and encourage each other in the journey of faith. And this community has its doors and windows open to the world. In fact, this community is scattered in the neighborhood, schools, and places of work for the purposes of blessing the wider community, and being heralds of God's *shalom*.

To move from consumer church to this kind of servant church will require a great conversion. It will mean that we identify more deeply with the passion of God, and less with our own comforts. It will mean that we discard the ethic of convenience, and enter new places of prayer and supplication.

Reflection: What needs to happen in me to make me open for such a commitment and lifestyle?

FROM THE LEAST OF THESE

Jesse had seven of his sons pass before Samuel, but Samuel said to him, "The Lord has not chosen these." So he asked Jesse, "Are these all the sons you have?" "There is still the youngest" Jesse answered . . . . So he sent and had him brought in . . . Then the Lord said, "Rise and anoint him, he is the one."

1 Samuel 16:10-12

It is important that we recognize, honor, and celebrate the many wise men and women in the life of the church, in religious orders, in para-church organizations, and in the general community, who in their maturity are there as faithful guides, and as signposts of hope.

From them we can learn much. And blessed is the person who has such a man or a woman as a spiritual director.

But over time such outstanding people rise to positions of leadership and responsibility. They become centrally located in the organizations and institutions they seek to serve. This is a wonderful opportunity for them to serve the community in a broader way. But this may also bring limitations.

All organizations have their goals, values and ethos, and leaders are called to serve those goals. Over time, this may begin to blunt their individual creativity. Moreover, leaders run the risk of over-believing their own abilities, strengths and rhetoric. As a result, they may cease to grow and develop.

It is therefore, not surprising that while God uses mature women and men, God also calls the unlikely ones from the margins to proclaim his wisdom.

St. Benedict in a basic and sober statement makes the observation that, "God often inspires the youngest to make the best suggestions," This empowering statement, of course, will only have relevance if such inputs from the least are listened to and acted upon.

Here lies our biggest challenge. In many communities of faith and Christian organizations, the least in the organizational structure have no voice. We so often are not a community of equals in Christ, even though the gospel calls us to recognize this, since Christ has broken down the social barriers that divide.

To the degree that we marginalize ordinary members, the young, the poor, and those with disability, and create structures of the powerful and efficient, we will hamper the mysterious and transformative work of God amongst us.

It is not for nothing that the gospel constantly holds up children as a metaphor of the wisdom of the Kingdom.

Our failure at this point simply shows the cultural captivity of the church, where it is more at home with the structures of power and efficiency, than with the structures of vulnerability.

Reflection: Are there places, where the voice of the least of these needs to be heard?

CHURCH:
A DIALECTIC RELATIONSHIP

You have heard that it was said, "Love your neighbor and hate your enemy." But I tell you: Love your enemies and pray for those who persecute you.

Matthew 5:43-44

There are some people who think that the best way that one can serve another person, or an institution, or a particular cause is by giving an unquestioning loyalty. This is thought to be the ultimate demonstration of faithfulness and commitment.

While this may seem to be laudable, it is essentially faulty and dangerous. Unquestioning loyalty can easily become a blinded faithfulness, and this can lead to sectarianism where one cooperates in maintaining a faulty tradition, or one cooperates in evil.

A healthy loyalty should never be unquestioning. It should be one of a critical faithfulness.

We see this in Jesus attitude towards the Jewish traditions of his time. He was both a faithful son of the Jewish faith, and a prophetic counter voice. He was the counter tenor of Judaism!

John Wesley reflects a similar posture. He comments, there are "two principles ... [the] first, I will not separate from the church ..., [and] secondly, in cases of necessity, I will vary from it."

This suggests and amazing dialectic, one of full participation, and one of deep questioning.

Sadly, our contemporary attitude towards the church, the community of faith, tends to be very different. We seem to lack a fundamental sense of commitment and loyalty. Ours is the era of consumer Christianity.

In moving towards a recovery of the importance of our commitment to Christ, as well as to the church as the body of Christ, the way forward is not to appeal to a new loyalty, but to a new found love.

True love for Christ involves true love of our brothers and sisters in the faith. It also involves love of neighbor, even of stranger and enemy.

Love of the community of faith, says, I will be there in good and difficult times. Love enters both into the joyful times in the life of the church, and into its failings and falterings.

Love knows stickability. But it also knows prophetic witness. However, the latter is only possible when love is bound to truth.

Prophetic witness is not primarily fault finding. It is calling the church to embrace more fully the gospel of the reign of God.

Challenging the present practice and ethos of the church must not come from a contrary spirit, but from a vision of the fullness of life in Christ in the community of faith.

True love is not blind. It is a love with heart, ears, and eyes open, not only to the condition of the church, but also to what God will yet do.

Reflection: How can we live this dialectic?

THE HEART OF
THE COMMUNITY

Do not offer the parts of your body to sin, as instruments of wickedness,
but rather offer yourselves to God, as those who have been brought from
death to life, and offer the parts of your body to him as instruments
of righteousness.

Romans 6:13

The transformative work of Christ, and the renewing presence
of the Spirit, make us different from the main ethos of our
culture, where individualism, self-sufficiency, and independence
are celebrated. This does not mean that the work of Christ makes
us weak and dependent. Rather, God's renewing work makes us
dependent on God, and available for service to others. In other
words, we are drawn from the myth of self-sufficiency into a life
of mutuality and sharing.

This life together, where we join in common celebration,
learning, sacrament, fellowship and service, is something we need
to grow into, for it stands in stark contrast to the values of our
time. As a result, we need to undergo an on-going conversion.
In discovering Christ, we need to discover and outwork a new
relationship to brothers and sisters in the journey of faith.

Jean Vanier, the founder of the L'Arche communities that serve
people with disabilities, knows something of this conversion. As
a result, he speaks of community as the "place of loss, a place of
conflict, a place of death, but it is also a place of resurrection."

For some, this may be surprising language. Is sharing in community not the place of blessing and encouragement? Is it not the place where we are strengthened? Of course, the answer to this is "yes." Community can be all of this and more for each of us.

But community is not *only* this. The above blessings are usually the fruit that comes from painful transformations. Therefore, community is not only the place of blessing. It is also the place of pain. It is the place where we are transformed.

And personal change never comes easily and without cost. It is not easy for us to commit ourselves to a group of people, some of whom we would never choose as friends. Nor is it always easy to lovingly give ourselves in service to others.

But community may be even more challenging. Are we willing to remain in a particular Christian community when the development of our professional career calls us elsewhere? Are we also willing to share housing and resources? And are we willing to open our community to serve the poor?

These are difficult matters, and call us to the kind of "death" that Vanier is talking about. It involves the conversion of our heart, and our economics. And it calls us to downward mobility, and the way of the cross.

But the way of the cross is also the way of new life. In living in solidarity with each other by the grace of Christ, we are changed more fully into the heart and passion of God. And in the vulnerability of our life together, we may experience the benediction of the God who calls us into relationship, mutuality, and care.

Reflection: Am I willing to be converted from the dominant values of my culture to the humility of the cross of Christ?

HEALING

GROWTH IN WHOLENESS

THE HEALING ADVENTURE

If my people, who are called by my name, will humble themselves and pray and seek my face and turn from their wicked ways, then I will hear from heaven and will forgive their sin and will heal their land.

2 Chronicles 7:14

Healing is hardly a sub-theme in the Christian story. God's salvation in Christ involves healing, mending, and renewal.

The challenge facing the contemporary church is to recover a full-orbed vision of God's healing activity beyond the therapeutic paradigm, and the excesses of some healing ministries. The problem with both of these concerns is that healing is seen solely in personal terms and as a faith demand.

Healing is basically not about bringing relief, but draws us more deeply into the life in God. It expresses God's mending activity in our lives, our communities, and in our world. Francis Meehan rightly points out that "we are never healed or connected totally unless our relationships to others as well as our relations to the world and its history are healed."

Many inter-related themes can be identified in the healing adventure. The first and most fundamental may be called spiritual healing. Here we are referring to the reparation of humanity's broken relationship with God as creator and redeemer. This is the beginning of a life of faith. It is entering into the life of Christ by the power of the Spirit. No greater healing can occur than the restoration of our relationship with God. All other forms of Christian healing are premised on this basic healing. And as we grow in our life with God its healing power will impact other dimensions of life.

We can further speak about the healing of human relationships. This is the horizontal outworking of our vertical restoration in God. Here we have in focus the building of Christian community, and the work of peacemaking and reconciliation. Spiritual friendship and mentoring, and all activities that build the social fabric of the human community, are also dimensions of this theme.

Physical healing, inner healing (the healing of our inner woundedness), and the healing of the demonized (those experiencing Satanic oppression) are further ways in which we can experience the renewing activity of the Spirit in our lives.

Finally, we can speak of social healing where we are set free from the dominant psycho-pathologies of our society and culture, and of ecological healing where we express a responsible stewardship of God's good earth.

God invites us into the richness of the Trinitarian life. From this welcome and embrace healing spills out in many directions. God's redemptive activity and healing embrace empowers us to become signposts and servants of God's transformative concern for the whole fabric of life.

Reflection: Identify where God's mending activity has occurred in your life, and where it further needs to take place?

REDEEMING THE PAST

For this is what the high and lofty One says—he who lives forever, whose name is holy: "I live in a high and holy place, but also with him who is contrite and lowly in spirit, to revive the spirit of the lowly and to revive the heart of the contrite."

Isaiah 57:15

We are the sum total of the whole of our past. Past experiences with their mix of blessings, failures and difficulties, have indelibly forged us into the persons that we now are. Thankfully, it is not simply the past that shapes our ongoing journey. We are also people of a future hope looking forward to what God will yet do in us and through us.

While there is much in our past that needs to be celebrated, there may also be matters that need resolution because we continue to carry pains that affect us for the worse. This may be seen in our present behaviors. Bernard Malamud speaks of one of his characters where "the past was a wound in the head."

Being thankful for the past, of course, does not mean being only thankful for the good things that have come our way. Trials and difficulties, and even failures, can be molded redemptively by God's formative hand. But deep woundedness springing from rejection, fear, or abuse can hardly serve us well.

The ever-present temptation will always be to deny, suppress, or to rationalize our woundedness. And various forms of compensatory behavior usually follow quickly on the heels of the above. But the challenge is to stop running—to face our woundedness and seek God's healing grace.

This is the invitation to walk the way of humility. It is also to walk the path of faith, trusting that the God of all grace and consolation will draw near to us with his forgiving grace, and his renewing power.

While we can open the wounds of the past to God in prayer as we become aware of unresolved issues, it is often necessary for us to receive the help and ministry of others. This requires great humility on our part. Things that have shamed and hurt us are usually things that we want to keep hidden. But even the very act of opening our issues to another person, in a prayerful setting, is already the beginning of the healing process.

Woundedness does not simply come from abuse, but also from neglect. The long and lonely years of lack of affirmation and care can leave us deeply hurting. While neglect cannot be readily undone, God's healing presence can bring relief to its sting in the embrace of his grace.

As we forgive those who have neglected or hurt us, bitterness is removed, and the gentle river of God's love can wash away the fears, disappointments, and pains.

Reflection: Are there areas of woundedness in my life that need to be visited by God's healing presence?

CHRISTIAN UNITY

I have given them the glory that you gave me, that they may be one as we are one: I in them and you in me. May they be brought to complete unity to let the world know that you sent me.

John 17:22-23

While the gifts of relationship and community continue in our world, we are also acutely aware of their frequent fragility, and their sometimes absence. In fact, much of our social fabric seems badly torn. Ethnic jealousies continue, the fear of the stranger is all too apparent, families break down, and relationships fall into disrepair.

In this kind of a world, a divided Christian church is hardly a beacon of light and a sign that things can be better. Instead, the church often reflects the same tribalism that scars the delicate fabric of society.

Into this state of affairs the words of Pope John XXIII come with simplicity and clarity: "let us seek that which unites us and not that which divides." And there is indeed much that the Christian communions have in common. The same Bible, the Apostolic Creeds, a common two-thousand-year journey of the Christian church, and the common exemplary figures of the faith. Who, for example, cannot gain inspiration from a St. Augustine, a St. John of the Cross, a Martin Luther, a John Wesley, a Mother Teresa, an Oscar Romero?

But much more fundamentally, the churches have in common a God who created, upholds and redeems the world. This Trinitarian

God: Father, Son and Holy Spirit, is persistent in love, gracious in mercy, and passionate in justice. This God is committed to the work of transformation, renewal and healing. This God is revealed in the face of Jesus Christ, and is present amongst us in the power of the Holy Spirit.

What the churches have in common is that they are all missionized by God. Invited to his grace. Welcome at his banqueting table. They are forgiven sinners celebrating the goodness and beneficence of their God.

We all share the common invitation to participate in the gifts of new life in Christ. The death and resurrection of Christ has opened the doors of friendship with God, forgiveness of sins, the renewal of our inner being, and has given us a new purpose and direction for our lives. Now we no longer live by the tired values of our world, but in the light of God's Kingdom of grace and peace.

Furthermore, the churches share a common calling to serve the world in witness, care, healing and transformation. God's desire is that all should come to his banqueting table. And so we are invited by God to tell the world that the doors are open, grace is extended, new life is offered.

Finally, as brothers and sisters in Christ, we are all empowered by the Spirit. The Spirit upholds and renews us. The Spirit pours out gifts of prophecy, healing, wisdom upon the people of God irrespective of whether one in Roman Catholic, Baptist, or Pentecostal.

So we do have much in common. Far more than we often realize. So let us then serve this God, and bless our world in his name.

Reflection: How may we make our unity in the common love for God, and our desire to see the world made whole in the grace of God, more fully visible?

THE PRACTICE OF LOVE

This is how we know what love is: Jesus Christ laid down his life for us. And we ought to lay down our lives for our brothers.

1 John 3:16

We in the First World live in an age of great sentimentality. Living in a society of plenty and shaped by urban realities, we have become "soft" and know little of the toughness of life. Sadly, our much-having has not made us more grateful, but more demanding.

This shaping of our lives by a culture of safety and excess, has spilled over into our understanding and experience of the Gospel. Christianity has become the religion of security and blessedness. And most of the church's teaching in the West makes Jesus the happy "add-on" to our lives. We have much, and also have God and all his benefits.

But at the heart of the Christian message there lies not a sentimentality of safety and happiness, but a scandal. In the Gospel we are invited to meet the suffering God. The God, who made the heavens and the earth, and who is all powerful and all knowing, in Christ, embraces the scandal of rejection, suffering, and a cruel death on the hill of abandonment.

While Christ's death and resurrection give us the fruit of life, since in his abandonment we are made welcome at God's banqueting table, we are also invited to bear his shame, and to enter his suffering. In the faithful following of Jesus there is not only the blessings of his grace, but also the cost of discipleship.

91

F. Dostoevsky reminds us that "love in action is a harsh and dreadful thing compared with love in dreams." In dreams we so often sentimentalize. Love is warm and wonderful. In love we are fulfilled. Love makes us happy.

But to love another person in real life involves commitment and sacrifice. And this is as true of our love for God, as it is of our love of neighbor.

To embrace God's love means that we join God in his passionate concern for our world. To love God is to join him in his mission of reconciliation, mercy, peace, and justice.

To love the neighbor may well call us to sacrifice, service, and care. And particularly to love the poor neighbor may call us to solidarity, downward mobility, and advocacy.

How harsh and purged would be the contours of our love, if we in the plentiful West, would truly serve our brothers and sisters in Christ in the poverty-stricken Third World? How that would purify our love! How it would move us from sentimentality to a love that knows how to walk the road of fellowship with the suffering Christ! And in this, would we not become more whole?

Reflection: In what ways does our love need to be purified?

A LOVE THAT SEES

So Jacob served seven years to get Rachel, but they seemed like only a few days to him because of his love for her.

Genesis 29:20

There are many kinds of love. The accepting love of a young child towards his or her parents. The caring love of parents for their children. The bonded love of siblings for each other. The national love one has for one's country. The committed and passionate love one has for one's lover.

And as diverse as one's relationships, and as varied as one's interests, we can also speak of the love among friends, and the love of learning, or the love of nature.

In the midst of all this diversity, we need to recognize that love has many contours. It is expressed in many differing ways, and it possesses many qualities.

One of love's qualities is to see the lovability of the other. This is supremely expressed in the way that God, the creator and redeemer, views us his creatures. Created to glorify God, yet steeped in our own willful waywardness, God views us not from the distance of disdain and disappointment. God sees us with a love that draws, and embraces us. And so God lavishes his love, care, and beneficence upon us.

God's love is a love that sees beyond the immediate to the core of who we are, and what we can become. It's a love that draws us forward.

This kind of love can also come to expression at the interpersonal level. W. B. Yeats expresses this well, "but one man loved the pilgrim soul in you, and loved the sorrows of your changing face." A love that sees both the visionary soul, and the pain and fragility of the other, is a love that does not seek to control. Instead, it is a love of wonder and appreciation. It is this kind of love that needs to grow in us, for so often the love we have for the other can be self-seeking and manipulative.

This accepting and appreciative love is one that celebrates the uniqueness of the other. It enters and marvels. It sees and identifies. It joins in order to encourage and empower.

The heart of Christian love, *agape*, is a love that is there *for* the other. It seeks to give. It wants to serve. It endeavors to protect. It strains to nurture. And it wants to do this not in a controlling or smothering way, but only in response to the openness of other.

Love sees what others often cannot see. It looks not simply at the outer person, and its beauty, or the lack thereof. It looks at the inner person, and sees its potentiality, and its woundedness. And in seeing does not flee or attempt to remake the other. But it stays long enough to be close, to care, and to empower.

Reflection: Who do I need to see with new eyes?

OF AND NOT OF THIS WORLD

My prayer is not that you take them out of the world but that you protect them from the evil one. They are not of the world, even as I am not of it.

John 17:15-16

For much of the Christian story, that is, of the church in history, an unfortunate dualism has marred the delicate texture of the pattern of the life of faith in the world. Influenced by the idea that the soul was more important than the body, there developed the idea of two classes of Christians. The one, part of the parish church, were people who married, were involved in agriculture and commerce, and were engaged in activities in the general society. They sustained their life of faith through the sacraments, teaching and nurture of the church, and through personal piety.

But there was another class of Christians who were regarded as superior. These were the monastics living a life of celibacy, poverty, and obedience. Their priority was a life of prayer sustained within a community of brothers or sisters.

Eusebius described these two ways of life as follows: "the one is above common human living; it admits not marriage, property, nor wealth but wholly separate from the customary life of man devotes itself to service of God alone in heavenly love. The other life, more humble and more human permits men to marry, have children, undertake office, command soldiers fighting in a good cause, attend to farming, trade and other secondary interests."

The recognition that there are two differing callings is helpful. But that the one is more *spiritual* than the other, has had unfortunate consequences throughout church history.

Surprisingly, in some contemporary Christian circles this kind of dualism is alive and well. As a result, a kind of vocational hierarchy is still in force. At the top rung of the ladder is the overseas missionary, followed by the para-church faith worker, with pastor or priest next in the picking order. Then follows all those working in the field of human services such as doctors, nurses and social workers. Farmers and small business people follow next. While those working in politics, media and financial institutions are somewhere towards the lower rungs of this spurious spiritual ladder.

This kind of thinking fragments God's concern for our world, in that it makes some areas of life more important than others. It also fragments the Christian community, in that it places certain ministries and areas of work above others. It furthermore fragments Christian spirituality. Certain ways of being and acting in the world are held to be more pleasing to God.

In contrast to this kind of thinking, we need to reaffirm God as creator and redeemer, God's love for the world and church. The challenge is to live to the glory of God in all the spheres of life, including not only the church or human services, but also the media, the arts, and the world of economics.

The amazing mosaic of life with its spirituality, sexuality and economics, with its creativity and maintenance, with its family and social structures, is best integrated not by dualistic thinking, but by a vision that serves all of life.

Reflection: In what ways are the traces of dualism still operating in my life?

PRAYER

ECHOES OF THE LONGING HEART

THE LONGING HEART

As the deer pants for streams of water, so my soul pants for you, O God. My soul thirsts for God, for the living God. When can I go and meet with God?

Psalm 42:1-2

The longing heart is the problematical heart. This is not simply because it recognizes areas of lack and unfulfillment, but because it frequently does not know how and where those needs may be met. Moreover, the greater the longing the greater its possible unfulfillment. This may bring sadness, and even despair.

Victor Hugo once wrote, "What we lack attracts us. Nobody loves the light like the blind man." And while the longing for the healing light may be ever so appropriate, this blessing may not always be given.

So how may we shelter, nurture, and care for the longing heart? How may it be directed and guided?

The longing heart is fundamental to our creatureliness. Made in the image of God, we have been richly endowed with the common gifts of God's beneficence. And in Christ we are graced with the blessings of salvation, and the endowment of the Spirit. As a result of these blessings, there is movement within our being. We aspire after the greater good. We have within us hidden treasure that strains to see the light of day.

But the longing heart is also the product of our falleness. We have lost the primal innocence of the Garden of Eden. We were made for God, yet have wandered so far. And even though in Christ we have come close to the Father heart of God, we are

99

far from God's eschatological fulfillment. Neither we ourselves, nor our relationships and communities, nor our world, has yet come into the fullness of life that God has promised. Thus we are pilgrims still far from our final homecoming.

Since the longing heart is not only the product of God's creativity, but also of our falleness, the longing heart will always be a divided heart. It aspires after God and God's good, but it can also be self-seeking. It can long for the good, but may find inappropriate ways to achieve it. It may long to love, but it may love wrongly.

Moreover, the longing heart may become the impatient heart. When needs and desires are not met by our demands on God's gracious care, we can begin to look elsewhere. Thus idolatry is always a temptation for the longing heart, and despair and complaint, may never be far from us.

The longing heart is thus the vulnerable heart that needs to be carefully guarded in the shelter of God's care, and in our deep surrender to the wisdom of God. There the longing heart can become the productive place for the fruit of God's Spirit.

Reflection: So what about my longing heart? What is it longing for?

THE YEARNING HEART

A longing fulfilled is sweet to the soul.

Proverbs 13:19a

There is a fundamental restlessness in the human being. In that restlessness we long for something better, more beautiful, and more whole. Most often, we have no real idea what that might look like.

One indicator of this restlessness is our frequent boredom. While we might initially become enchanted with something or someone, it usually does not take too long before a dulling ordinariness begins to set in.

One does not need to be a social prophet to realize that this restlessness can easily become misused and exploited. Capitalist society is particularly expert at exploitation. It constantly suggests to us that our restlessness is due to our not having enough, and then goes on propose the better paying career, the fancy new car, or the exotic holiday. In the West, the preferred solution to our restlessness is more material benefits. Sadly, many of us live this twisted answer, even though we question it. And Christians are no exception to this point. They too believe that true life means having more of God's blessings and goodness. And this is often understood in material terms.

So what do we do with this restlessness, and the yearnings of the human heart? St. Augustine recognised this as fundamental to the human condition and suggests that "we move forward not with steps, but with yearnings."

But, if we want to move forward with these yearnings of ours, we need to put them in safe hands, and move in an appropriate direction. For we know, all too readily, how our yearnings can lead us in wrong directions, and can disempower rather than empower us.

Yearnings need to be handed over to God since our ultimate yearnings for wholeness can only be met from God's beneficent hand. God alone is truly there for us in his grace and mercy. God alone through his transformative work can make us new. And God alone will journey with us into the wholeness of life in the eschatological future.

Our other, and more secondary yearnings, also need to be handed over to God as we seek his will for us in all things. And this has implications for where we live, the choice of a career, the friendships we make, the priorities we set, and the orientation and texture of our lives.

In the ultimate yearnings of the soul we look for new heavens and a new earth. In our more intermediate yearnings we long for more of God's kingdom amongst us, for greater love and integrity, and a more persistent way in serving others, including the stranger who so easily recedes from our view.

Reflection: What are my deepest yearnings, and where are they directed?

WATCHMEN

Son of man, I have made you a watchman for the house of Israel; so hear the word I speak and give them warning for me.

Ezekiel 33:7

Our contemporary society does not encourage us to be gazers, but to be doers. In our Western capitalist market economy, productivity is valued. While the East has greater resources for spiritual reflection, this too is threatened by the global economy. As a result, everything else becomes peripheral to the human enterprise of working and producing.

But our world not only needs doers, but also dreamers and visionaries. And we need these both within the wider society as well as within the communities of faith. In society, dreamers can begin to articulate a more authentic vision of life and community. And in the church, visionaries can open up for us new ways of understanding and responding to God, and working that out in greater service to the world.

The church in its long march in history has had a tradition of producing seers and visionaries. Generally speaking, these have not been the ecclesiastics of the church. Their concerns have had much more to do with the provision of religious services for the faithful, and the maintenance of the church and its related institutions such as schools and facilities of care.

Seers have often come from the periphery of the church, particularly in the form of reformers and those committed to renewal. But seers and visionaries have also come from monasteries where in a life of prayer and reflection the new breath of the Spirit has brought life, hope, and renewal.

In the liturgical cycle of daily prayers monks were like watchmen looking to God while the rest of the world slept. In early mornings over centuries, monks were awake, prayerful, watching-looking to the God of grace to guard and protect, and to renew and empower his people. In faith, they prayed that the powers of darkness be diminished, that the face of the earth be fructified, and that humanity would know the face of God. In the words of Thomas Merton, they were "planted like sentinels upon the world's frontier."

In our time of religious uncertainty, in this post-Christendom age, we need to recapture the art of waiting, and to emulate the ministry of watchmen. Our desacralized world does not, first of all, need the ministry of our evangelical activism. It needs the plaintive cry of God's people. It needs the women and men who will, in prayer, probe the heart of God, while discerning the heart of the world.

But watchmen are not passive waiters. There is no resignation about them, nor cynicism. Instead, they are women and men of faith and hope looking to the God of the exile to bring redemption to our broken world.

While the world sleeps the sleep of restless forgetfulness, God's people are called to be awake, to watch, to pray, and to hope that the God of the heavens and of history will grace the world with his renewing presence and embrace humanity in the *shalom* of his Kingdom.

Reflection: In what ways can I deepen the discipline of prayer in spite of the many pressures and responsibilities that demand my time and attention?

TRUE SPIRITUALITY

Righteous and justice are the foundation of your throne; love and faithfulness go before you. Blessed are those who have learned to acclaim you, who walk in the light of your presence, O LORD.

Psalm 89:14-15

Spirituality has nothing to do with self-preoccupation. Nor is it mere inwardness. Evelyn Underhill puts this well: "still less does the spiritual life mean a mere cultivation of one's soul; poking about our interior premises with an electric torch."

Sometimes we erroneously get the impression that spirituality only involves the development of the inner life, and that it necessitates our withdrawal from ordinary life. Hence the contemplative monk becomes the main model for true spirituality.

This understanding of the spiritual life is one sided. Spirituality is far more all embracing than the practices of asceticism and introspection.

Christian spirituality does not have its starting point in what we are, but in who God is, and in God's recreative work in our lives leading to a life of wonder, worship and service. Thus spirituality does not simply involve the exercise of certain practices such as prayer and meditation, but the way in which we live the whole of our lives in and with God, and in our world.

True spirituality has its genesis in the transformation that God's work of grace brings about in our lives. And this spirituality is sustained by the ongoing work of the Spirit in our hearts, life-style, and values.

We grow in spirituality not simply through certain disciplines—as important as these are—but through the outpouring of God's *shalom* upon us, our participation in family, church, and workplace, and through all the bitter-sweet experiences of life that form and shape us. Spirituality is thus formed not only within sanctuary, but in all the joys and responsibilities of life, as we live the gospel, and are sustained by the Spirit.

The spiritual disciplines of prayer, reflection, asceticism, the meditative reading of Scripture, and participating in sacramental life, all help to sustain and deepen our awareness of God's presence. But these disciplines of themselves cannot give the life that only God can give.

Thus true spirituality is the life we live in God, and for the purposes of his Kingdom. Thus spirituality will always lead to service and witness. Enamoured with God, we seek to bless the neighbor in whom we can barely see the hidden face of Christ.

Reflection: Does love of God and love of neighbor come to expression in my spirituality?

PRAYER: AN UNVEILING

Surely you desire truth in the inner parts; you teach me wisdom in the inmost place.

Psalm 51:6

Prayer is the bread and butter of Christian spirituality. To be a Christian means that one is a person of prayer.

Prayer as the heartbeat of the spiritual life comes in many forms, and occurs in every setting of life.

There are prayers of adoration and praise. There are prayers of petition and prayers of intercession. There are prayers of worship and prayers of lament; prayers of thanksgiving and, yes, prayers of complaint.

And prayer can take place in all the circumstances and situations of our life: the sanctuary, the workplace, the home.

But prayer is not only an activity. It is also a process. And one key process in the act of prayer is a gentle unveiling.

Don Saliers has put this well. To pray, he notes, is to "encounter the ambiguous reality of our own humanity before God." Or to put the same sense in different words: prayer is the unmasking of the false self through the discovery of the true self in the face of Jesus Christ.

There are many dimensions to this process of unveiling in the discipline of prayer.

The most basic is that in prayer we acknowledge our creatureliness in the presence of the God who made the heavens and the earth, who loves us, and seeks to make covenant with us. In prayer we recognize that God is God, and we are not.

But prayer is also an expression of friendship and relationship. It is the joy of being with God. It is happiness in the presence of the God who welcomes us in Jesus Christ, and who graces us with the nearness of the Holy Spirit.

Prayer, however, can also be a disturbing experience. Prayer can be, and frequently is, transformational. In prayer we discover things about ourselves that we have neglected, or ignored, or suppressed. This discovery is not the fruit of our own psychologizing, but is the blessing of the God who reveals himself, and in whose presence and light we are unveiled.

While this may sound scary we should remember both the firmness and gentleness of God.

The purpose of unveiling in God's presence has nothing to do with condemnation, but has everything to do with invitation. Our false self is revealed in order that we may more fully move towards conformity in Christ.

To discover ourselves in the presence of God is to be reminded of God's love for us in creation and redemption. It is to rediscover that God is the center of our lives and that life with him, in him, and through him, is life indeed.

Prayer that transforms us is the blessing of prayer.

Reflection: How can I pray in ways that call me to greater openness?

ATTENTIVENESS

THE ART OF CONTEMPLATION

THE LISTENING HEART

The Lord came and stood there, calling as at other times, "Samuel! Samuel!" Then Samuel said, "Speak for your servant is listening."

1 Samuel 3:10

As contemporary global Christians we should not be so enamoured with the rationalism and scientism of our age that we think that God can only speak to us in prepositional terms. God can speak to us in the circumstances of our lives, in the depths of our heart, through the witness of another person, and in mysterious forms of revelation. But God does want to speak to us through his Word by his Spirit.

However, how we approach God's Word does have something to do with the way God speaks. If we only come to Scripture with our particular interpretive strategies to exploit the Bible for scholarly purposes, then the Bible may be helpful to describe an ancient world, but mute as a word that speaks to the core of our existence.

If we wish to approach the Bible in terms of its transforming power, rather than through the use of instrumental reason, we would do well to rediscover the ancient church tradition of *lectio divina*. This is a way of reading Scripture that speaks to the deep needs of our life. This much slower way of reading the Bible can help us to become more attentive to the living voice of God—a voice we need so much to hear in our sterile and empty world so devoid of meaning and hope.

This reading of Scripture lingers at a particular passage and waits to hear a specific word—a word that brings hope, or challenge, or direction, or comfort. This word then becomes the focus of our attention. We think about and reflect on that word or phrase (*meditatio*).

In prayer *(oratio)*, we then talk with God about this word. We ask for further insight, we ask for faith to believe, and for courage to respond. We pray for God's light to shine upon us, and for our hearts to be enlarged and our horizons expanded.

This highly interactive and dynamic process leads to *contemplatio* where we sit with what we believe that God has spoken to our hearts. And we are open to God's presence permeating our being.

In traditional evangelical circles where so much is made of reading Scripture, usually with the help of a Bible commentary on a particular book, *lectio divina* may well be an *additional* discipline which can deepen our listening and hearing of Scripture.

This practice is important for the time in which we live, where preaching has become primarily psychological, personal Scripture reading is mainly for comfort, where theology is only for scholars and not the laity, and where our lives are simply too full and busy for quiet reflection. It is particularly important because we need to recover a confidence in the written Word, and in the belief that God wishes to be with us and speak to us.

Sadly, as contemporary Christians we are in many ways spiritual orphans. God seems so absent from our world, and often from our lives. In the quiet place, the place of prayer, and in the meditative reading of Scripture, we are invited to recover a sense of connectedness with the God who has welcomed us into his embrace.

Reflection: Can I move slower and become more attentive in order to be more deeply nourished?

FIRST THINGS FIRST

*Come, let us bow down in worship, let us kneel before the Lord our
Maker; for he is our God and we are the people of his pasture, the
flock under his care.*

Psalm 95:6-7

L iving in the modern world, it is very easy for us to get things
back to front. Our culture lauds productivity. The God of the
Bible, however, calls us first to receptivity. Our culture stresses
individualism. The biblical story invites us into community. Many
other comparisons could be made.

But where we possibly get things most badly out of kilter is in
the activism that subverts our praying. While some mainstream
Protestant churches have become social welfare "clubs" with little
emphasis on discipleship in Christ and empowerment in the Spirit,
evangelical churches are hardly centers of spirituality. They have
become known for their activism and busyness.

While in no way wanting to make little of the importance
of service and mission, there are fundamental realities of the
Christian life that should not become neglected. The most basic,
besides a life of worship, is the practice of prayer. And P. T. Forsyth
emphasizes this with crystal clarity: "it is truer to say that we live
the Christian life in order to pray, than that we pray in order to
live the Christian life."

Prayer so easily becomes a matter of instrumentality. We pray in
order to get certain results. We pray in order to get what we want.
And while it is appropriate to make our own needs, and the needs

of others known to God, this is not the heart of the mystery of prayer in Christian experience.

Prayer lies at the heart of the Christian experience, because the Christian life is an echo of the heart of God. And key to the movement between God and the human being, and the human being and God, is a mutual song.

God says welcome. And we come. God gives us gifts. And we worship the giver. God sends forth his Spirit. And we worship our Creator and Redeemer in spirit and truth. God speaks. And we utter responses in prayer and adoration.

Prayer is, therefore, our grateful response to the presence and movement of God in our lives. It is a song of the heart. The hello of the Spirit. It is our "yes" to the "yes" of God.

Prayer is, therefore, a communion. A communion between God and creature. And while our creaturehood emphasizes the great gulf, communion emphasizes the great friendship that exists between God and us.

Prayer, as a result, is God's invitation and our response. In prayer, God inhabits us and we inhabit God. Thus in God we dwell in the house of prayer. This house is not a temple, but our very being in communion with the God of grace. To dwell there is worship, well-being and empowerment. For the God who dwells with us makes us whole and calls us into the world.

Reflection: How can prayer become communion rather than mere asking?

BEING PRESENT TO

When Jesus reached the spot, he looked up and said to him, "Zacchaeus, come down immediately. I must stay at your house today."

Luke 19:5

Relationships form the very fabric of our existence. Our very genesis is the fruit of a relationship of great intimacy. We are nurtured and cared for during our time of delicate vulnerability by those who brought us into being. And in the continuation of our life journey many others enter our lives—siblings, members of our wider family, neighbors, teachers, colleagues and friends.

In all of these relationships we both give and receive, and the quality of this receiving and giving weaves the very texture of our being. Our very being, character and personality, while formed by our genetic inheritance, is shaped by both the beauty and pain of these relationships.

It is the miracle of life, and a sign of God's grace, that it is not only the strength of these relationships that forms us, but also the failure that is ever present. Out of woundedness certain gifts emerge. But this is only possible if we are not overcome by anger and bitterness. Thus woundedness embalmed in the oil of forgiveness becomes the seedbed for the growth of the Spirit.

Sadly, while we recognize the critical importance of meaningful relationships, our contemporary Western culture is not particularly good at fostering relationships. We are simply too individualistically and programmatically driven. Even in our doing things *for* others, we often do not know very well how to be *with* them.

Jean Vanier, the founder of the L'Arche communities, providing care for intellectually and physically disabled persons, makes the careful observation that "to love someone is not first of all to do things for them, but to reveal to them their beauty and value."

At the heart of relationships lie, first of all, not the matter of much doing, even though serving the other is so important. Instead, relationships are birthed in contemplation. They arise out of an ability to see what others may not see, or what the person himself or herself cannot believe is true of them.

Contemplation involves being present to. But this is not any kind of presence. It is the presence of love which allows us to see truly. To see truly is to see not only what is there but is so often hidden, but to see what is potentially there. Thus it is a seeing in hope. It is eschatological and visionary. It sees what will yet come to be, and calls this forward and into being.

In this sense relationships are so empowering because they move us from where we are to where we can be.

Reflection: Can you identify and celebrate a person who has been so present and empowering to you?

THE PRACTICE OF SILENCE

*I would flee far away and stay in the desert; I would hurry to my place
of shelter, far from the tempest and storm.*

Psalm 55:7-8

Ours has become a culture of instant availability through ever
more sophisticated means of communication technology. In
many ways this is good. It is efficient for business, and it is good
for education and interpersonal communication. And in times of
emergency, it saves lives.

But a healthy rhythm of life is never one that only engages. We
must also practice the art of withdrawal. And in that withdrawal
we have the opportunity to return to an inner silence.

Inner silence has become a rare commodity in our kind of
world. And even in the practice of the church, silence is an all but
forgotten discipline. We are ever so busy with liturgy, sacraments,
preaching and sharing. All of this is good. But silence is no
luxury.

Henri Nouwen believes that the practice of silence affirms us in
our pilgrim status, and "guards the fire within" our hearts from
which all speaking must come. Let me elaborate in my own words
what that may mean.

Being alone gives us the opportunity of moving to stillness and
solitude. In this movement we become aware of the fact that not
everything we have and do is all that important. Moreover, we
may become aware that not everything here satisfies and fulfills us.
This draws us to God in prayer and contemplation. And in God's

presence we become aware that we belong to another Kingdom, and that finally we are strangers here.

This being with God in solitude and contemplation nurtures an inner sacredness. Our secret does not lie in our achievements, but in our friendship with God. What is seen by others around us does not explain all that we are. There is an inner life with God, nurtured by the Spirit, that is the great secret of one's existence.

Out of this inner sacredness sustained and guarded by God, I may live, act, and speak. And this will give my acting and speaking an authenticity, freshness, and creativity.

Things then do not come from empty wells, tired places, and the barren and wounded spaces of our lives. Things do not come from mere repetition of the boringly familiar and artificial. Instead, they come from the sacred silences that characterize our lives.

Contemporary Christian spirituality urgently needs to recover the places of shelter in God's presence where true communion and empowerment can occur.

Reflection: What of your inner sacred spaces? What do they look like?

DRINK DEEPLY!

Then Jesus declared, "I am the bread of life. He who comes to me will never go hungry and he who believes in me will never be thirsty."

John 6:35

For several hundred years since the Enlightenment, the idea of a separation between the sacred and the secular has steadily grown in Western, and now in global culture. And with this has come the notion that the secular world is the world of rational and scientific certainty, and therefore the world of dependability. The sacred world, on the other hand, is seen as the world of subjective preference. It is not infrequently seen as the world of superstition.

It is rather obvious from the above that the secular world is seen as superior to that of the sacred. And even though in the world of the twenty-first century, the optimistic view of scientific rationalism is deeply questioned, we are still enamoured with our ability to solve our problems through technical know-how.

As Christians living in the modern world, there is much that we can celebrate. Science and technology have brought us many benefits. But we need to be careful that we don't live the sacred-secular divide. In other words, we need to watch that we do not regard the sacred as the optional extra.

The Christian life does not have God as a stop gap for problems we cannot solve ourselves. God is at the center. We seek to live all of life in God's presence, and under his benediction.

Moreover, God is not only relevant for the spiritual dimensions of life, such as prayer. God is also important for our daily lives: for politics, the arts, and economics. With God at the center all of life finds meaning in him.

The above comments have implications for a life of professional Christian service. It is ever so easy in our preaching, teaching, and pastoral care, or in our service to a needy world, that we practically live the sacred-secular divide. What I mean by this is, that we use worldly strategies to achieve spiritual outcomes, or that we do much our activity without being prayerful or committed to nourishing our inner being.

Eugene Peterson rightly warns us: "if the word is pushed out of the way and made servant to action and program, we lose connection with the vast interior springs of redemption which come out of the word, the word made flesh."

Prayer and service, and contemplation and action, need to be held together. Our daily life and our life with God need to interpenetrate. In this way, we live beyond the sacred-secular divide in that all of life is important, and all of life is to be lived with and before God.

As contemporary Christians we don't want to fall into a deadening pragmatism. Nor do we want to embrace a world-denying piety. Instead, we seek to glorify God in all things.

Reflection: In what ways do I still live the sacred-secular divide, and how can I overcome this?

A SUBVERSIVE READING
OF SCRIPTURE

Here is my servant, whom I uphold, my chosen one in whom I delight;
I will put my Spirit on him and he will bring justice to the nations.

Isaiah 42:1

We can approach Scripture in many different ways. The Bible can be read for its stories about the ancient world. It can also be read for its moral wisdom. Furthermore, it can be read for its literary and poetic beauty.

This in no way exhausts all the possibilities. The theologian may read the Bible to construct theological propositions, and the linguist may become absorbed by the particularities of its language and phrasing.

To read Scripture in these ways does not fully do justice to the way that Scripture should be read. The Bible is not simply a book for our interest and exploration.

What is of greater general concern, however, is that so many Christians not only do not read Scripture, but when they do they read it basically as a comfort book. In our therapeutic culture the Bible acts more as a pill to aleviate our pains and concerns. It is hardly read as God's transformative Word to us, let alone, read for its subversive values of God's upside-down kingdom.

William Stringfellow in his reading of Scripture wrote, "I look for style not stereotype, for precedent not model, for parable not proposition, for analogue not aphorism, for paradox not syllogism,

121

for signs not statutes." Here is an attempt to read Scripture without seeking to fit it into our Western rational categories.

But there are deeper ways of reading Scripture.

The most profound has to do with the realization that the Bible is not there as a book of stories and ideas for us to exploit and mine. The issue is not what we do with the Bible, but what it does with us. The Bible is God's living and transformative Word to us. God addresses us. We are confronted, and called by its wisdom and power. We are exposed by its light, and called to surrender.

In Scripture we are invited to the embrace and healing presence of God. We are called to inhabit its stories, imbibe its insights, and to live by its vision of grandeur of who God is and all that he will do.

At the same time, we are invited to understand and participate in its subversive nature. The Bible turns our world upside down. Forgiveness, not self-seeking power is the way to life. Servanthood, not exploitation is the way to serve others. Greatness is humility. Transformation comes through a cross, not through might and splendor.

Throughout its pages, we can read of God's heart for the poor, his concern for justice, the power of community, the significance of prayer, the relevance of relinquishment, and the meaning of love.

This book cannot be read simply to reinforce our concerns. Rather, it calls us to embrace the concerns of the creator and redeemer of this world.

Reflection: Are there ways of reading the Bible afresh as God's address to me?

FORGIVENESS
EXTENDING GRACE

THE ART OF CONFESSION

Therefore confess your sins to each other and pray for each other so that you may be healed.

James 5:16

There are several important elements without which a meaningful and wholesome life would not be possible. A number of valued relationships is one of them. Good vocational choices is another. Some may want to highlight other important dimensions of life.

The giving and receiving of forgiveness is clearly one other important aspect of life. This is so, because we readily fail others, and others also sin against us. More importantly, we also sin against God's holiness and beneficence.

Forgiveness involves the art of confession. I call it an art because it needs to be couched in the wisdom of discernment. This is so because, while I always need to forgive, I need to be discerning as to whom I make my confession.

So do I make my confession of my failure or wrong doing to God alone, or also to the person I have wronged, or do I make it to God but in the presence of another person? There are no simple rules to guide us regarding these matters.

What is clear is that I should always make confession to God. For even when my sin is against the neighbor, I have violated God's instruction to live in love towards the neighbor.

What is less clear is that I should always confess to the one I have failed or wronged. This is particularly difficult when that person

125

may not be aware of what I have done, or when my confession may involve divulging things about others.

But what is singularly challenging is when I know that I should confess my sins to God in the presence of another person. Dietrich Bonhoeffer once made the observation that it is "in confession that we affirm and accept our cross." Or to put that differently, in such a confession we embrace the death of humility.

To lay ourselves open before God and another person, while painful and humiliating, may also become the place of deep healing for us. Our very transparency can break the bonds of darkness that may have encased a particular situation. And the words of forgiveness and peace that we hear from the brother or sister in whose presence we have confessed can bring renewal, hope, and healing.

The paradox of life is that the place of vulnerability is the place of strength; the place of humility, healing; and the place of death, a resurrection reality. Therefore, while it is true that confession is to embrace the cross, it is more so the embrace of God's gift of new life.

Confession of sins, therefore, belongs to the order of resurrection. It is the lightness of healing for the heaviest burden.

Reflection: Around what issues do I need to walk the road of confessional humility?

DEALING WITH OUR WOUNDEDNESS

And by his wounds we are healed.

Isaiah 53:5b

We experience both the goodness of our world and of all human relationships, and we experience disappointments and pain. For some goodness predominates. For others pain is the major melody.

What finally shapes the major contours of our being is not what we do with the goodness that comes our way, but how we respond to life's difficulties and disappointments.

Our response to suffering will more fundamentally determine our character, than how we have responded when the winds have blown favorably, and the gentle rains have brought forth a good harvest.

Suffering and difficulties are the crucibles for our formation.

Richard Rohr is therefore to the point when he reminds us that "you either transform your pain or you transmit it."

I think we all know something about the doubtful art of transmission. We tell others about how so and so has harmed, hurt, or betrayed us. We draw others into the circle of our hurt and woundedness. And over time this may well become a wide circle of anger and bitterness.

The gentle, but challenging art of transformation, is usually something we do less well. It is in living out this artistic vision that we need all the help and inspiration we can possibly get! And it is an art, for it springs from our imagination touched by the biblical vision.

Transforming rather than transmitting our pain calls for a radical reorientation to what comes most naturally. When we hurt we wish to retaliate. We want to hit back.

However, to forgive those who have wounded us, and to lay down anger and hatred, and not to hold anything against the one who has hurt us, is to undergo a deep conversion. This is following the way of Christ. And this way is lived by the sustaining grace of God.

The sweet music of forgiveness is good news not only to the wrongdoer, but also to the inner person of the one wronged. This music dispels the timbrals of darkness.

Forgiveness is but the first step in this transformative process. To allow a painful experience to purge us is a further step. And to live in goodness towards others as a result of what we have learned is another way of living our forgiveness.

The work for justice so often comes from those who have taken these initial steps on the road of transformation. To work for justice is to bless others who have been sinned against. Thus great fruit can come from a woundedness that is not allowed to fester, but becomes the womb of reconciliation.

Reflection: Identify an experience where your hurt became productive for others.

TRANSFORMATION

Do not conform any longer to the pattern of this world, but be transformed by the renewing of your mind.

Romans 12:2a

Albert Einstein once made the observation that "no problem can be solved by the same consciousness that caused it." This is an important and radical insight, and relates to the idea of a paradigm shift.

Living within the framework of a particular set of social and cultural values, we are more shaped by our environment than we are prepared to admit. Thus we imbibe ideas and values, and circulate and promote them. As such, we may uncritically promote what is far from good.

What is necessary in order to break with the flow and continuity of tradition, is for a rupture to occur. This rupture can take many forms. One of the most basic is when we see the long term unintended, but unhelpful and destructive consequences of particular ideas, values, and strategies.

Seeing what we do to others that hurts and harms can call us to a deep conversion and transformation. It can cause us to seek forgiveness for the harm done, and to bring forth fruits of repentance.

That we do, at times, harm others is basic, though unfortunate, to the human condition. That we harm others when we did not intend to do so is a sobering and humbling lesson, and opens up an awareness of the fragility and complexity of human existence.

In the family sphere we know something about this. Well-meaning and generous hearted parents do not always do good to their children. They may well make them irresponsible, or spoil them.

In the community of faith well meaning clergy and other church workers may promote a form of Christianity that is about receiving, but knows little of serving.

And in the wider political arena we know of liberation movements that have brought about newer and sometimes greater forms of oppression.

We need to repent not only of harm done, but also of good not done or not done well. And we need to repent of actions well meant that have had unintended consequences.

This calls us to a radical humility. It calls for a renewal of heart and mind. It calls us to see things in a different light.

To seek forgiveness is to move from harming to blessing. And sometimes those who seek to do good need the deepest conversion.

Transformation is not only for the missionized, but also for the missioner.

Reflection: In what ways do I need to be converted from doing "good"?

THE DOUBLE WOUND

You were taught, with regard to your former way of life, to put off your old self, which is being corrupted by its deceitful desires; to be made new in the attitude of your minds; and to put on the new self, created to be like God in true righteousness and holiness.

Ephesians 4:22-24

While we may quest for wholeness and integration, the human condition is characterized by fragmentation and alienation. At the theological level, we have lost the Garden of Eden and are still far from God's eschatological future. At the creational level, we are wrenched from our mother's womb and never truly find home again. And at the existential level, we live with the aching disparity between our hopes and dreams, and the beautiful and pungent reality of life.

What adds to the intrigue and difficulty of the human drama is the sense that there are larger factors that constantly impact our lives. We are subject to the powers. We may not have the same sense about these powers as our forebears, with their fear of the forces of nature and the elemental spirits of the universe. But we are all too aware of the powers of persuasion, ideology, technology, and of the psychic forces that disturb our inner world and play havoc in our relationships and social landscape. We are not as free as we would like to believe ourselves to be!

Jacques Maritain is all too aware of these realities and notes that the human being "is out of joint and wounded—wounded by the devil with the wound of concupiscence and by God's wound

131

of love." Thus, it is not only the powers of our social reality that impact, thwart and mould us, but there are also transcendental powers that infiltrate our very existence.

Our contemporary folly is that we deny this double woundedness. With an optimistic humanism, we reject the power of evil. And with a self-sufficient individualism, we reject our need for God's grace.

The biblical story, however, sketches with broad strokes of the brush that we are subject not only to our personal weaknesses and sins, nor only to the forces of nature and the powers of our social world, but also to the transcendental powers of good and evil. These powers of light and darkness are not to be seen as a balanced dualism. The woundedness that springs from God's love, which strikes us at the very core of our waywardness, futility and arrogance, is a wound that calls us to the God who embraces us in grace and mercy. This wound is one that turns us into a new direction. And this wound will always be greater than the one that deepens our alienation, folly, and despair.

The wound of God's love, the fruit of the suffering God in Christ Jesus, calls us home to God's healing. The wound of concupiscence, deepens our darkness, and leaves us homeless and in deeper pain.

Reflection: How can we more fully embrace God's wound of love that brings healing and salvation?

RELINQUISHMENT

LIVING WITH OPEN HANDS

ENTERING THE DESERT

*Jesus, full of the Holy Spirit, returned from the Jordan and was led
by the Spirit in the desert, where for forty days he was tempted by the
devil.*

Luke 4:1-2

The experience of the desert has long been a theme of Christian
spirituality. Israel's experience of the long years in the
wilderness marked it as a place of judgement and purification.
Jesus' desert experience was the precursor for the annunciation
of the Kingdom of God. And for the Desert Fathers, the desert
became the place of renunciation, mortification, and prayer.

Shaped by these primal paradigms, the desert has featured as
a key metaphor in the experience of the Christian life. Christian
experience is not simply one of green pastures and flowing
streams, it is also the place of emptiness. While God's banquet
table is spread out for the sons and daughters of the Kingdom of
Heaven, God's children are also invited to dark and lonely places
in their experience of the grace of God.

While some Christians only wish to emphasize the Promised
Land as the central feature of Christian experience, a more balanced
understanding of Christian spirituality includes the experience of
the desert. This far more adequately reflects "the yet" and "not yet"
nature of our participation in God's Kingdom. Moreover, it more
accurately reflects the death and resurrection motif, which lies at
the very heart of the Christian story and Christian experience. In
the place of darkness, God's light shines. In the desolate place, we

135

experience God's friendship. The empty hands are the ones that God fills with good things.

The desert as a metaphor of Christian experience may involve the dark night of the soul, the art of relinquishment, and the experience of the silence of God's presence. But as Segundo Galilea has pointed out, the notion of the desert also has implications for the missional work of the church in societal transformation. We are called to resist all that is unjust in our society. In "the desert of critical detachment," prophetic engagement becomes a possibility.

The desert thus also stands as a symbol of detachment. In the practice of the art of disengagement, we can begin to see the major contours of our society in a new light. This needs to be done in the light of God's Word, and in the spirit of prayer.

Fruitful engagement, sustained service, and transformative action in our world, must pass through the crucible of the desert experience. It is there that we can be stripped of our illusions, identify our idolatries, and be gripped by a renewed vision of God's upside-down kingdom.

Those who only want the promised land and the banqueting table, will know nothing of the mystery of God who makes weakness strength, and fills our emptiness.

Reflection: Identify your experience of the desert, and celebrate the fruit it has brought forth.

LIVING FOR GOD'S GLORY

But you are a chosen people, a royal priesthood, a holy nation, a people belonging to God, that you may declare the praises of him who called you out of darkness into his wonderful light.

1 Peter 2:9

There have been times in the history of the Christian church when the idea was prevalent that one had to live a very special life in order to live to God's glory. For some, that meant living in the desert. For others, it involved becoming a monk.

While some of this was motivated by a genuine desire to live a life of faithfulness and commitment, this was often mixed with an unhealthy dualism.

In some ways, that dualism is still alive today, in that we tend to think more highly of a Christian missionary working amongst a foreign people, than we do of a Christian working at the stock exchange.

But this dualism is not found in the biblical story. There is no elevation of the soul over the body, and the whole of life is to be lived under Christ's lordship. Thus in our relationships, within our families, in our daily work, and as part of the institutions where we serve, we seek to be servants of God.

But at the same time, there is a challenge for us contemporary Christians posed by those living an ascetic lifestyle. In the words of John Chrysostom: "those who live in the world even though married, ought to resemble the monks in everything else." In other words, there are things in the commitment and lifestyle of monks that those of us, who live the Christian life in the daily realities of our world, could imitate.

I see three important lessons that we can learn.

The first, has to do with the practice of building Christian community. Monks were part of a brotherhood or sisterhood in Christ. They lived in intentional community. We live in a time of consumer Christianity, and commuter churches. We know little about deep relationships in Christ, and this has all sorts of negative implications for our growth in faith and discipleship. We urgently need to recover ways to live life together in Christ.

Secondly, monks lived a rhythm of prayer. Built into the fabric of each day was the discipline of prayer and reflection. In living our busy and distracted lifestyles we need to recover a daily pattern of prayer, silence, and worship, in order to be more fully present to the God of all grace.

And finally, monks practiced various forms of asceticism. They said "no" to certain good things in life. We, who live in a consumer society where we are always questing for more, need to find this grace for ourselves. We need to find the ability to say "no," so we can more fully say "yes" to God.

Reflection: Where do I need to say "no,'" in order to open greater spaces for the presence of God?

THOSE UNCERTAIN RICHES

Two things I ask of you, O Lᴏʀᴅ; do not refuse me before I die: Keep falsehood and lies far from me, give me neither poverty nor riches, but give me only my daily bread.

Proverbs 30:7-8

The biblical picture regarding material possessions is clear and unambiguous. The God who has created all things, has provided for us, through the resources of the earth and through the labor of our hands, so that we should have enough. It is also clear that we are called not to live for our possessions. Rather, we are invited to make God and his concerns the central focus of our lives, and to be grateful for the material blessings that come our way. Moreover, the Bible is clear that what we have is never simply for ourselves. We are part of the Body of Christ and of the human community, and are invited to share with those who are in need.

But the matter of material possessions has become problematic for us. We live in a world of gross imbalances. Not only is there dire poverty in much of the world, and the gap between the First and Third world continues to widen, but also within the First World poverty is a chronic reality.

That we are all influenced by the secular gospel of much-having is everywhere evident. To have many possessions, we are told, shapes our identity, and guarantees our status in society. Moreover, to have much is never enough, and so we attempt to feed an insatiable desire for more.

139

This secular gospel has also made its inroads into the community of faith. The gospel of prosperity and the idea that God is there to give us all that we desire, continues in its appeal.

In the light of these realities, it seems to me that the contemporary church needs to rediscover a spirituality of asceticism and new forms of solidarity with the poor.

St. John of the Cross once made the comment, "there are two ways to be rich: to have everything or to want nothing." It is the latter statement that begins to point us towards a spirituality of asceticism. This has nothing to do with a spirituality that seeks to earn credit in the heavenly ledger. But it has everything to do with living out of a new center.

When God is our dwelling place, and God's concerns become ours, then we will seek to live God's *shalom* towards others. Our identity is then found in God and not in what we have, and as a consequence, what we have becomes the basis for thankfulness and generous sharing.

A spirituality of asceticism will lead us to joining with the poor and needy, so that they too can rejoice in God's care and provision.

Reflection: Is a redefinition of our lifestyle called for in the light of the Gospel?

CREATING SUBSTITUTES

My people have committed two sins: They have forsaken me the spring of living water, and have dug their own cisterns, broken cisterns that cannot hold water.

Jeremiah 2:13

The human being exists with awesome potentialities. As the creature willed by God, we have been blessed with great capacities, which can be expressed within the framework of our free response to God.

What is clear from the biblical story is that we are wonderfully made, but are called to outwork our giftedness within the setting of God's covenant with us. Created to live in God, we are called to live for God within the community of his people as those who live under his Word as worshippers and obedient followers. And from this center, we are called to live for God in serving the neighbor, and transforming our world.

That this vision of life is not held by all is everywhere writ large on the pages of history. The human story is as much a flight from God as it is a movement towards God. Human beings have used their amazing capacities as much for themselves, or for wrong causes, as they have been used for God's peaceable kingdom.

But the problem of the human story is not only a matter of flight from the presence of God, it is also a matter of creating other Gods. Karl Barth has rightly pointed out that "the human being is an *idolorum fabrica*"—an idol factory.

Idolatry is not simply a problem of the ancient world. And even though we moderns may dismiss it as a superstitious practice of the hoary past, it is a fundamental human problem. This is so, since if it is true that we are made for God to live in his presence, our flight from God will inevitably lead us to the creation of spiritual substitutes.

Simply put, if God is not our highest concern, value, and focus, then whatever else is that concern will take on the specter of idolatry. And the gods that we create, whether that be national military might or the personal pursuit of wealth and status, are gods that we will readily cling to even though they are the gods that fail. We find it ever so difficult to relinquish the work of our hands, particularly when that work has been forged out of our own rebellion.

Creating our own gods is the ultimate form of a self-deluding self-assertion. This partakes of the same folly as the person who has himself or herself for a doctor or mentor. Such a person has a fool for a doctor or guide!

Reflection: Is God the center out of whom I live, or are there also other gods?

CALLING

LIVING OBEDIENCE

A SENSE OF DESTINY
AND CALLING

*For we do not preach ourselves, but Jesus Christ as Lord, and ourselves
as your servants for Jesus' sake.*

2 Corinthians 4:5

As Christians in the Western world we are living in difficult
times. The difficulty has nothing to do with the lack of
economic well-being, and general political freedoms. Although I
must hasten to add that increasing numbers of people in the First
World are living Fourth World realities due to marginalization,
lack of employment, and the inappropriate use of technology in
putting ever greater constraints on personal freedoms.

But I have other difficulties in view. My main concern is that
the greatly weakened church in the West is failing to form and
shape women and men of commitment, dedication, and vision.
This is partly due to the fact that the church has become culturally
captive. In our pluralistic and relativistic world it is simply
unacceptable to believe anything so deeply that one is willing to
order one's life accordingly. This is regarded as fanaticism, and
being blinded by ideology.

If truth and certainty are no longer possibilities, then a strong
commitment to anything is no longer possible as well. Although it
is ironic that in the West we don't live this consistently. While we
believe that religious truth is mere personal opinion, we continue
to live the "truth" of progress, self-interest and prosperity.

But the gospel cannot be lived in some half-hearted way. The
message of Christ's death bringing new life is not good news for

145

the peripheral aspects of our life. It's a message that strikes to the core of who we are, and reorients us to live with and for God and his Kingdom of peace and justice.

It's a gospel that permeates the very fabric of our being, our priorities, and values. It calls us to prayer, contemplation, and service. It invites us to abandon our petty concerns and our self-preoccupations, and to live God's *shalom* in the here and now.

The gospel is not an invitation to live a narrow bigotry and fanaticism. But it does invite us to live a life of conformity to Christ, and to enter into the suffering of humanity.

This kind of commitment was true already of the teenage Dietrich Bonhoeffer. When his family ridiculed his desire to study theology and serve the church in the world, he responded "if the church is feeble, I shall reform it." While this was a somewhat pretentious statement, Bonhoeffer, captivated by the Sermon on the Mount, lived and died to serve Christ, and the community of faith.

The challenge facing us Christians in the West is to recover a profound spirituality, a radical obedience, and a willingness to serve Christ in the church and in the world at the cost of our own empty pursuits.

This commitment does not come from the will to power. It can only come from being transformed by the love of God, and by being empowered by his Word and Spirit.

This is not so much a call for the emergence of great men and women. It is only the call to a deeper conversion.

Reflection: In what ways can I become more fully a person of the Kingdom of God?

GOD'S STRANGE WAYS

Amos answered Amaziah, "I was neither a prophet nor a prophet's son, but I was a shepherd, and I also took care of sycamore-fig trees. But the LORD took me from tending the flock and said to me, 'Go prophesy to my people Israel.'"

Amos 7:14-15

It is obvious that God uses men and women who serve him in traditional religious roles. In the Old Testament priests, prophets, and kings were all servants of Yahweh. And in the New Testament apostles, elders, deacons, and pastors served the purposes of the risen Christ.

But it seems that God has a certain fondness in catching us unawares, and turning traditional roles upside down. One way in which this occurs is when God calls the unlikely to be his spokespersons.

This God did with Amos.

Priscilla, a woman of faith, surprisingly also received a call to leadership in one of the house churches of early Christianity (1 Corinthians 16:19).

God also called the unlikely journalist, Dorothy Day, to be his servant to the poor, and God's witness to peace. Day does not mince her words when she talks about the God of surprises. She comments: "the mass bourgeois smug Christians who denied Christ in his poor, made me turn to Communism. And it was the Communists and working with them, that made me turn to God."

147

The fact that God calls people in unconventional ways, and calls the most unlikely, is a signal for all of us in the household of faith to be open to the strange workings of God. And to be humble about our part in the great purposes of God.

The Kingdom of God is not in our hands. The working of the Spirit is not under our control. The power of the gospel is not ours to unleash. And the spiritual transformation of another person is not what we can do.

We are only servants of the Reign of God. We are mere witnesses.

The power lies with God. And God is at work in the world his wonders to perform.

One of the wonders of God are those whom he calls and chooses. Abram. Jacob. Job. David. Matthew. Phoebe. And the unlikely Dorothy Day whose commitment to the simplicity of the Gospel made her a voice for the poor, for justice, and for peace.

God is able to turn a foe into a friend. A coward into a prophet. A harlot into a servant of Christ.

While we may celebrate the God of predictability, the God of reversal is the God who calls us to follow him. He makes the strong weak, and exalts the poor. This God calls us. So let us be open to all that God may do and say.

Reflection: How can we be open to God's unusual ways?

POSSESSIONS

*All the believers were together and had everything in common. Selling
their possessions and goods, they gave to anyone as he had need.*

Acts 2:44-45

Most of us in the modern world live in societies and economies
where private ownership is fostered and encouraged. In
Australia, the dream of owning your own home set on decent
suburban block of land, persists.

In the West, the idea of private ownership is often overlaid
with notions of much having and prosperity. It almost seems as
if enough is never enough. And so the quest for having more is
something that begins to possess us. It is almost as if we no longer
possess our possessions, but that they possess us.

While the biblical tradition, and the story of Christians in
history, in no way contradicts the basic idea of private ownership
of property and goods, there are some powerful themes that
moderate and modify this key idea. The tribal ethic of Israel was
communally oriented. And Israel was called by Yahweh to have
in view the poor and the stranger. Both the Jerusalem church
and the Pauline house churches practiced sharing, not only of
spiritual rituals and disciplines, but also of goods and resources.
And throughout the long history of the church, various Christian
communities, including Monastic communities, practiced a
commonality of goods.

The radical wing of the Reformation, the Anabaptists, gave
much attention to the way in which the call of Jesus affected not

149

simply one's soul, but also one's praxis in relationships, community, work, and engagement with the world. They wrestled with what it meant to live a Messianic lifestyle.

At heart they believed that the call to discipleship involved following the suffering Christ into the world, living the Sermon on the Mount, living in community, sharing resources, and saying "no" to the powers of the age, including the powers of war and nationalism. They believed that Christians were to live a counter-cultural lifestyle.

One of their early leaders, Balthasar Hubmaier once stated "we are not the lords of our possessions, but stewards and distributors." This statement came out of a vision that Christ does not call us to an individualism, but to a form of communitarianism. Conversion is not only a transformation of the soul, but also affects the way we handle our money and possessions.

Implicit in Hubmaier's statement is the idea that what we have is not simply for ourselves. All we have comes from God's beneficence. God entrusts these good gifts to us in order that we might worship our Creator and Redeemer, bless those within our sphere of responsibility and care, and share with others, particularly those in need.

In living like this, we seek to demonstrate the kindness of God, and live beyond the power of possessions. This means that what is different about us is not simply that we name the name of Jesus and acknowledge him as lord, but also that we live differently with and towards what we have. In other words, spirituality has everything to do with economics.

Reflection: How can our attitude towards our possessions be converted?

MISSION

This is what the Sovereign Lord says to these bones: I will make breath enter you, and you will come to life.

Ezekiel 37:5

While we may wish that it was otherwise, we have to admit that mission does not come easy to us. In fact, most of us find it downright difficult. We are either afraid or uncertain about how to engage others in witness and service, or are too preoccupied with our own work, issues, and lifestyle. Generally speaking, Christians do not pour out their lives into the world in order to bless others.

And yet whether we like it or not, mission should not be peripheral to the Christian life. This is for several reasons. The first, is that God is a missionizing God. God reaches out into the world to sustain, welcome, renew, reconcile, and make us whole. Secondly, mission was central to the ministry of Jesus. Preaching the good news of the Kingdom, and healing the sick and demonized, Jesus served as a midwife to bring people into the grace and blessing of God.

In living and following in the ways of God, mission, therefore, should also be central to our lives. The surprise in the work of mission and ministry, is that we not only bless others, but we ourselves are also blessed. Ivan Illich puts this well, the outcome of mission for the church is "when her historical appearance is so new that she has to strain herself to recognize her past in the mirror of the present." Simply put, mission renews the face of the church, not only the face of the world.

This, of course, is not to suggest that the motivation and intent of mission is that we only should benefit. Far from it. It is exactly the opposite. Mission is cooperating in and with the passion of God for the transformation, renewal, and healing of our world. This involves doing God's good in our world so that people are made whole, communities are renewed, and the social order reflects more of God's shalom.

There is nothing narrow about our mission in the world, because God's mission is all embrasive. It is never simply soul saving. It is the blessing and renewal of the whole person. And it does not only have the individual in view, but persons in their contexts of family, institutions, and society. God's grace and healing power seek to renew all the dimensions of life.

But in the work of mission the church itself finds renewal and blessing. This is so for several reasons. The first, is that in mission the church resonates with the heartbeat of God. Secondly, in reaching beyond itself the church expresses a life-giving vitality. Thirdly, the church is blessed with the fruit of its mission when new people join and make their contribution to the community of faith. And finally, in seeking to be missionally relevant, the church will need to find new ways of configuring its life together as a community of faith. This also, will bless the church.

Reflection: How can we serve the world more fully so that we also can be more fully enriched?

ASCETICISM

Then he called the crowd to him along with his disciples and said: "If anyone would come after me, he must deny himself and take up his cross and follow me."

Mark 8:34

The Christian life is the amazing movement of celebrating life, and the practice of self-denial. The one is as important as the other. In celebration, we acknowledge the goodness of God. In self-denial, we follow the suffering Christ into the world as healers and peacemakers.

Unlike the church in the Third World which already suffers so much due to the dire poverty of many of its members, the communities of faith in the First World know little of the practice of asceticism and relinquishment. In fact, the Western church is largely captivated by the gospel of plenty, and the message of God's goodness has not been translated into a life of sacrificial service.

The challenge facing the church in the West lies in its need to resist the powers of this age, and to become more deeply rooted in the biblical story, in a life of prayer, and the practice of asceticism. Thomas Merton points us towards his own tradition in responding to these matters. He writes: "it is of the very essence of the monastic life to protest by its simplicity and liberty against these servitudes."

The monastic life is a significant illustration of our need to say both "yes" and "no." Yes, to a life of worship, prayer, work, and service. No, to the powerful seductive forces in our contemporary world that trumpet the message of much-having and consumerism. In fact, we are promised by our culture that we can have and experience everything. At a price, of course!

There are other and equally significant examples of Christians living a lifestyle that reflects the values of the gospel, and that run counter to the dominant values of our time.

Some of my friends have deliberately chosen a life of downward mobility, others serve the poor, others have relocated themselves in needy neighborhoods, others have downscaled their spending and now live much simpler lifestyles. Others again, now serve in Third World contexts. The examples are endless.

But the point is clear. These are all forms of asceticism. They involve the willing opening and emptying of our hands. They involve a letting go of things that our consumer culture suggests we should hold on to.

The blessings of asceticism are varied and many. These include the smile of God regarding our acts of obedience and service. They include the blessing of empty spaces that God can fill, and the grace of vulnerability and humility as we open our hearts and hands.

Asceticism reminds us of our poverty before God. It reminds us of those who, through no fault of their own, have so little. Moreover, asceticism draws us into fellowship with the humiliated and suffering Christ whose power blossomed in the face of great shame and rejection.

Thus asceticism is no duty. It is certainly not a way to gain God's blessing. God's blessings are freely given. But asceticism is the surprising blessing for those who open their hearts and their hands.

Reflection: Where do I need to open my hands?

FAULTY BURDENS

The Lord is my shepherd, I shall not be in want. He makes me lie down in green pastures, he leads me besides quiet waters, he restores my soul.

Psalm 23:1-3a

I think that it is more than a little sad that Christians sometimes make God out to be a tyrant. They see the Christian life as being hard and demanding. They often speak of the cross, but hardly ever of the resurrection. And they give the impression that God only demands service and sacrifice, and gives little by way of joy and blessing.

This tainted perspective occurs amongst Christians who are doing the hard work of urban mission, and the work of justice and transformation. Overwhelmed by needs, problems and challenges, and often not understood and supported by their brothers and sisters in the faith, they feel abandoned. As a result, God becomes the target of their hurt.

This scenario offers many challenges, including the embrace of a realism that stops us from taking on more than we can cope with. It also challenges us to rethink the way in which we go about our work where we pile more and more on our shoulders, but fail to draw others in to what we are doing. Or to put that even more strongly, we fail to delegate to others, and thereby, do not empower the wider community regarding their engagement and participation.

But Thomas Merton has rightly identified an even more basic issue. He points out that when we lose our spirituality in our service we become "a beast of burden." A focus on doing, without a corresponding emphasis on being nurtured, is ultimately deadly to our sense of identity, well-being, and the quality of our service.

In the rush of an activism that is often configured more by our own compulsions, our need to be needed, and our own do-gooderism, we fail to hear what God is saying to us and asking of us. Moreover, in our busy response to great need, we fail to embrace personal limitation. Furthermore, in our busy serving we often attempt to live off the memory of God's presence and grace, and not out of the present reality of God's nurture and care.

Service that is not grounded in and sustained by a spirituality rooted in the presence of the Spirit, the gift of the Eucharist, the practice of prayer, and solitude and contemplation, is a service that soon becomes tired or twisted. Moreover, it overlooks the fact that our greatest gift to others is not our frenetic activism, but the gift of love, friendship, time, and companionship. In other words, the greatest gift is not our gifts, but ourselves.

Hence, if we only have a frazzled self to give, we give very little. So finally, we in the West with our messianic complex and fix-it mentality need to learn to pray more and do less. We need to become less busy and more faithful; more self-giving and less oriented to giving things.

Reflection: How can I grow deeper in God so that my serving comes from the overflow of God's presence and blessing?

156

JOURNEYING

FOLLOWING THE GOD OF SURPRISES

THE CALL OF THE UNFAMILIAR

So after I have completed this task and have made sure that they have received this fruit, I will go to Spain and visit you on the way. I know that when I come to you, I will come in the full measure of the blessing of Christ.

Romans 15:28-29

Our life is formed well in the network of secure and loving relationships, and in the places of familiarity. Place and relationality form our soulscapes.

I still carry with me both the warmth of wider family, the familiar scenes of the small Northern Holland town of Franeker, the experience of Christian community, and the exotic diversity of the sub-tropical rainforests of the Lamington Plateau in Southern Queensland, Australia.

Familiar relationships and places play a formative, as well as a stabilizing role, in our lives. And in this, they prepare us to move beyond what we know and have. The familiar becomes the basis from which to pursue the unfamiliar. Stability need not become the place of boredom and unfreedom, but can be the seedbed for adventure.

Lichtenberg once made the statement, "I would like to become unfamiliar with everything in order to see again." The author is right in the desire to see life with new eyes. How freeing and invigorating that can be. The familiar can become so dull and this dullness becomes the lens through which we see and process the new.

As a result, the new is stripped of its newness as it becomes assimilated with our familiarity.

But the familiar should not be discarded. We cannot leave ourselves behind. Instead, the familiar may be the place from which we engage the unfamiliar, providing we do not elevate the familiar and negate the unfamiliar.

From the love and security of what we have and know, we can engage the other—whether that be a new person, culture or set of ideas—with an openness that can only enrich us. So we bring the old to the new for the former's transformation.

This movement from the old to the new makes life rich. But this does not mean that the new is always better. Always, some of the old will be retained, and sometimes some of the new will need to be discarded.

This dialectic of life has relevance for our emotional and social growth and development. It is also at the heart of the Christian missional experience where we move from our familiar places to incarnate ourselves in the unfamiliar in our service for Christ. There also we cannot discard the old and "go native." But in order to truly serve those to whom we are called, we appreciate the new and allow it to open up for us wider understandings of what is means to be human. It allows us to appreciate the amazing riches of the grace and creativity of the God, who both inhabits the old and the new, and is beyond everything.

Reflection: How have I been enriched by moving beyond the familiar?

PUSHING THE BOUNDARIES

The Lord had said to Abram, "Leave your country, your people and your father's household and go to the land I will show you."

Genesis 12:1

There is a very basic rhythm of life: being secure and moving out to take on new challenges. There are many other word pictures we could use to describe this movement: being at home and being on the road; the work of consolidation and the challenge of expansion; being grounded and learning how to fly; cleaving and leaving.

We can most readily apply this movement of life to childhood experience with its security of the home preparing the child for the eventual transition into adulthood and leaving. The first movement, being at home, lays the basis for the second movement, moving out in order to create one's own home and context.

But this double movement of life does not occur only once. It takes place again and again as we respond to the new transition phases of our lives and to the new challenges that face us. All this occurs when, in the words of Joseph Campbell, "the familiar horizon has been outgrown."

While we can readily see how this movement is part of the transition to adulthood and part of the move from one career to another, we also need to discover this as part of the spiritual dimensions of life.

For some, this latter perspective may be a bit of a surprise since the spiritual dimension has to do with the discovery of the

161

ultimate reality. The question is then asked: How can one outgrow the ultimate?

The answer to this is that we grow in the spiritual life just as we develop in other aspects of life. And therefore we do outgrow the early and familiar horizons of our religious experience.

For some, this has meant the deepening of the particular Christian tradition of which they are a part. For others, this has resulted in embracing another theological perspective.

We should never forget that Jesus grew up as a faithful son of the Judaism of his day. But inspired by the will of his Father, and a vision of the Kingdom of God, Jesus pushed the boundaries and created the new.

The richness of the new that Jesus brought about is so vast and so deep that no single ecclesiastical tradition can contain it. And so while we need to be deeply grateful for the church that first nurtured us, just as we need to be grateful for the parental home that first succored us, we may well need to move on to find another ecclesial home.

I am not talking about the restless and useless search for the ideal Christian community. Nor is this a movement based on mere negation and rejection. Rather, its impulse is positive. It is the movement to growth, and to a further embrace of the God, who invites us to an ever deeper knowing and being loved.

Reflection: What gifts of security do I need to celebrate? And what challenges for change and transformation do I need to embrace?

BEYOND BALANCE

If we are distressed, it is for your comfort and salvation; if we are comforted, it is for your comfort, which produces in you patient endurance of the same sufferings we suffer.

2 Corinthians 1:6

There are a number of emphases in the contemporary church that continue to distort its life. One, has to do with the erroneous idea that the Christian life is basically a fair-weather experience. The other, is that living the Christian life is a matter of balance.

While different, the two notions are related in that, if one holds that the Christian life is the experience of what is good and whole and not what is troubling and difficult, then clearly one could argue that this is a matter of balance. I want to question this idea.

The Christian life is not a fair-weather experience, nor is it a life of balance. It is a life that knows both wholeness and brokenness, and failure and forgiveness. It knows both the graciousness of God, and the woundedness of our world. It is a life that is constantly reborn in the womb of hope, but it also knows the unanswered questions of life.

There is nothing neat and tidy about any of this. So, we can't really speak about balance. In fact, the metaphor of journey, and the notion of paradox, better typify the Christian life than any idea of balance.

The notion of balance has more a therapeutic, rather than a theological basis. The basic idea in the therapeutic model is that the Christian faith adds to and perfects our humanity. In Christ we become whole. God adds to what is lacking and thus we become more complete.

There is much truth in all of this. But this is not the whole story. Graced by God we remain sinners. And God does not simply add things to us, God also takes things away. Sometimes this is an awesome stripping process!

The *theological* basis of the Christian life is one that follows the paschal mystery. It speaks of the wonder of what God has done in Christ for the restoration of all things, but it also speaks of the narrow road, the discipline of God, the experience of suffering, and the reality of death.

We always need to remind ourselves that Jesus ended up on a cross. There is nothing balanced about that! And while there are times when God leads us besides still waters, there is also the experience of the desert. There are times of presence and absence. There are seasons of growth and pruning. There are the joyful blessings and the severe mercy.

Karl Rahner once paradoxically noted that "balance becomes a dropping of the balance." And so it is. There is nothing balanced about being in the place of prayer, nor about leaving one's family, friends, and familiar surroundings in response to God's call to serve elsewhere. There is nothing balanced about forgiving a person who has hurt us; nor in giving away a lot of your money.

The Christian life is not a fine balance, but living the mystery of the cross.

Reflection: What does living more of the paradox of the Christian life look like for me?

GENTLENESS

Why are you downcast, O my soul? Why so disturbed within me? Put your hope in God, for I will yet praise him, my Savior and my God.

Psalm 42:5

Our kind of world knows little about the playful art of gentleness. It seems to know much more about pushing and shoving in order to get ahead. Strenuous determination and even aggression are much more the marks of our contemporary world. After all, one has to get the market edge!

While in no way wanting to decry the importance of planning and hard work, the biblical picture of life emphasizes celebration as well as activity, Sabbath as well as the reality of work. Sadly, Christians often live more the cultural pattern of life than a biblical one.

I would like to highlight further that Christians are often the most driven and often the busiest in our society. This is so for a number of reasons. The first, is that Christians want the best of both worlds—the heavenly and the earthly Kingdom. So they work doubly hard, doing well in their jobs, as well as seeking to serve the church. Secondly, Christians are often guilt-ridden. They believe that they don't do enough to serve God and others, and thus they push themselves to assuage their guilt.

But to live well, it is imperative that we learn to be gentle with ourselves. Roman Guardini puts this well: the person "who wishes to advance must always being again ... Patience with oneself ... is the foundation of all progress."

165

We are invited to live this kind of gentleness for many reasons. One, has to do with the recognition that we can't make everything happen. We are dependent on others, and there is a time and season for most things. Secondly, we all run out of steam and lose our way. Thus we have to start again, sometimes at the very beginning.

But the more basic reason why we should be gentle with ourselves is because that is the way that God bends towards us. We are graced not dragged into the Kingdom. We are loved not forced onto the path of reconciliation and peace.

If God is gentle in his care for us, so we should be kind to ourselves, let alone to others. This gentleness towards ourselves has nothing to do with laziness, and is not the same as condoning what is unacceptable in our lifestyle and attitudes. It is all very different. Gentleness towards ourselves begins with the recognition that we are not God. It has to do with accepting limitation and allowing the contribution of others.

Moreover, gentleness frees us from the tyranny of ultimacy. It gives us the gift of experimentation where we are willing to try something new, but are also willing to relinquish the project when it becomes evident that it won't work.

Finally, gentleness walks the path of forgiveness where we not only forgive others for their faults, but ourselves as well, for our own stupidity.

Reflection: In what ways do I do violence to myself and others?

VULNERABILITY
RECOGNIZING OUR HUMANNESS

HUMAN FRAGILITY

All our days pass away under your wrath; we finish our years with a moan.

Psalm 90:9

Our very beginning is so inauspicious, and is ever so fragile. Formed from an act of love and hidden in the womb, we are conceived without our consent, Morris West reminds us, and 'wrenched whimpering into an alien universe with our death sentence already written on the palms of our helpless hands'.

That we die in a similarly fragile manner is a fact of human existence.

Between these two events of vulnerability—birth and death—we live life. Some live lives of greatness, others live a mediocrity, and some live lives of poverty and degradation.

For Christians, all of the above, is also true of them. They form no exception to life's fragile realities. Like others, they too are born into this world, and like others have to face the great exit. Some Christians rise to great social prominence, while many live lives of daily subsistence in a world characterized by injustice. This is particularly true of our Third World sisters and brothers.

In many ways, there is nothing magically different about Christian existence. And we need to be careful that we do not cast the experience of the Christian life in utopian categories. There are no magic escape routes for the Christian in the human fray.

Like others, Christians are thrown into the world, are sustained by it, are shaped by culture, and partake of the pain and beauty of our world.

The fact that the beginnings of our life and its finality are so fragile, is a signal that possibly the whole of life should be lived that way. That we tend *not* to live this way, however, is everywhere obvious. We want to hide our fragile selves and to make ourselves strong through position, status, and power. In fact, some people try to make themselves invincible.

Christians can also think this way. They believe that the Christian life is all about strength in God, empowerment by the Spirit, and gaining key positions in the church and in the world in order to be a power for good. While it is true that God does empower us, that it's good to be a blessing to the church and the world, and it's appropriate to rise to positions of leadership, this should come from an interiority of weakness and vulnerability.

The central motif of the Christian life is that we are dependent on God, and that in and of ourselves, we are not great. We are those who constantly need to receive God's grace and forgiveness. And we constantly need to resist the temptations of power in order to walk the road of humility, service, and relinquishment.

Fragility is a fact of our creatureliness. Fragility is, furthermore, a calling in our following of Jesus who went the way of cross.

While we may be out of step with others in society, we must not be afraid to live this way. For in God's upside-down kingdom the weak are strong, the poor are rich, those who pray have power, those who give are filled with good things, and those who walk the royal road of peace will disarm their enemies.

Reflection: Are the central motivations of my life those of control or those of relinquishment?

LIFE'S SOBER STORY

The length of our days is seventy years—or eighty, if we have the strength; yet their span is but trouble and sorrow, for they quickly pass, and we fly away.

Psalm 90:10

I would not say that I have lived a charmed life, but I have been incredibly blessed. I have a wonderful wife and family, have had the opportunity to work in various fields of endeavour, have lived on several continents, have been able to study, and have had wonderful openings for spiritual ministry and service.

This is not to say that there has not been a polyphony of difficulties: financial struggles, health issues, ministry and work problems, and failures and disappointments. But, in my case, the latter do not outweigh the former.

None of this is to suggest that life has always been full of excitement, challenge, and joy. This is simply not the case. Much of life has a mundane sameness about it, even when we seek daily to live our life with God through the empowerment of his Spirit. Thus Victor Hugo is right, "hours of ecstasy are never more than a moment."

But what deeply concerns me is that some people around me live a very different story. Theirs are stories of trouble and sorrow. Some are unmitigated disasters. And these are brothers and sisters in Christ! They are persons of quality and faith, and yet, life for them seems so hard and so cruel.

What are we to make of these realities? We can hardly turn a blind eye and pretend that these people do not exist. They are right here amongst us.

One very unhelpful way of responding is to suggest to these strugglers that God is somehow punishing them. I should not have to write this. But it is necessary. Some evangelicals are quick to see the judgment of God in the misfortune of others.

An equally unhelpful response is to suggest that we understand what they are going through. The truth is that we seldom do, for the journey of pain is the loneliest journey of all, upstaged only by the journey of death.

Furthermore, we may have to resist the faulty idea that we can fix things. Some persons' pain is not fixable. People with disabilities, the poor, and those experiencing injustice do not have problems that have ready solutions!

The most difficult pain that my friends experience is the pain inflicted upon them by their loved ones. Wayward children, for example, can cause untold pain for parents, siblings, and grandparents.

One response is prayerfully to accompany these friends of ours. When they have long given up hope, we who are not so emotionally involved can continue to have hope for them.

This is not to suggest that we pity them. This places us in a superior position. Companionship, faith, prayer and hope, and not pity, is what we are called to.

Moreover, this does not mean that we take no practical action. But we have to be careful that our actions are not unrealistic, and therefore, will only create further despair.

Reflection: How can I best enter another's pain?

ON DOUBLE WINGS

Teach us to number our days aright, that we may gain a heart of wisdom.

Psalm 90:12

Francois Mitterand once made the observation that "birth and death are the two wings of time." What we may want to make of this metaphor is up to our creative imagination. But I want to play with the idea that we should live our lives with both points of the continuum in view. As well, we are invited to embrace the idea that the cycles of birth and death occur *within* time and *within* the span of our lives.

To remember our birth is to celebrate the mystery of life, to see it as God's precious gift, and to appreciate our parents for their part in this most awesome of beginnings. Birth reminds us of the sheer fragility of the genesis of the human journey. It reminds us of the vulnerability of the human condition. The human person so in need of sustenance, care and shelter, so utterly dependent, so totally at the disposal of the generosity of others!

While birth brings us into time, death remains the certain but unknown termination of time. Death is the final boundary of our earthly existence. It is the all-powerful reminder that all things come to an end. It is the abyss that we all plunge into. Death is the final reminder of our creatureliness.

But it is within these two wings of time that we also experience the cycles of birth and death. We all know something of the movements of creative new life within us and the time it takes for that to come to expression and eventual fulfillment. And all of us have experienced the reality of letting go, of something being taken away, of dreams and projects deteriorating and dying.

Not only the human journey, but the whole movement of the created order manifests the cycle of birth and death. We see this in the seasons, in the rhythm of sowing and reaping, in the life cycle of subtropical rainforests, and in the very structure of ecosystems.

The Christian life begins with the birth of the life of God within us: the mysterious movements of the Spirit, the awakening of faith, the realization of our sinfulness and unworthiness, and the joy of recognition that God has provided for us in Christ and welcomes us into his embrace. These are some of the contours of this new beginning. And this beginning is not the end. God continues to birth new things in us. The creative Spirit, ever hovering and brooding, brings new life.

But death also occurs within the birthing of the new. Old values, idolatries and preoccupations need to be discarded and left behind. This is the death we often stubbornly resist, but need to embrace. The dying of the old so that the new may more fully emerge, is the cycle of the mystery of the Christian life.

In all of this, so much is out of our control that we are understandably afraid. But in God's careful hands we can find peace in this journey of renewal.

Reflection: Where are the birthing signs of something new in my life? And what needs to die off so that new life may more fully emerge?

LIVING THE DIALECTIC

Not only so, but we ourselves, who have the first fruits of the Spirit, groan inwardly as we wait eagerly for our adoption as sons, the redemption of our bodies.

Romans 8:23

While some Christians want to suggest that a fundamental peace should characterize the Christian experience, I believe that a basic restlessness is far more appropriate. This is so, because we live a life of faith and hope as we lean towards the future.

W. Manson once spoke of "the patient impatience of the Christian in hope." In this, he captures the basic dialectic of the Christian journey. We are patient because we believe in God's sovereignty. We are impatient because we live in the hope of what God will yet do.

This leaning towards the future does not mean that we do not commit ourselves to present tasks and projects. It has nothing to do with a life of irresponsibility. Nor does it mean that we always hang loose and can't make important decisions.

The opposite is in fact the case. The Christian life involves the saying of "yes." We say yes to God and his will and ways. And, therefore, we say yes to others as we make our commitments and fulfill our responsibilities. This saying yes occurs in the ordinary realities of life—marriage, work and government.

But the Christian life also has to do with saying "no." In God's upside-down Kingdom the obvious way is not necessarily the right way. And the way forward may be the way of relinquishment.

175

Moreover, saying a yes to God may well mean saying a no to other things.

God's good news involves not only annunciation, but also denunciation, where we identify and resist the powers of this age.

This restlessness at the heart of Christian experience, involving the saying of yes and no, does not mean that its source is frustration. Nor is it the product of anxiety or a life of striving. This restlessness comes from a very different place. It comes from being with the God who already inhabits the future and who is moving all things towards the great *eschaton*.

Put differently, being at peace with God does not mean that we become static, but dynamic. Right relationship with God gives us a tranquility, but not a passivity. For what we now desire is that others, and the whole of God's world, will also experience this *shalom*.

The challenge for us is that we enter the restlessness of God, who desires that all come to salvation and wholeness, that justice reigns, and that the whole earth be filled with peace.

Reflection: Have I become too accepting of the way things are, and no longer proactive in reaching for the future?

RADICAL FREEDOM

But now that you have been set free from sin and have become slaves to God, the benefit you reap leads to holiness, and the result is eternal life.

Romans 6:22

A strange paradox lies at the very heart of the human condition: there is the appropriate impulse towards freedom, but there is also the failure to understand the true nature of freedom and the way to achieve it. What this means, is that the very good we are seeking turns out to be so different and often the opposite of what we were looking for, because the quest for freedom comes from a wounded place.

Our woundedness, while person specific, is fundamentally archetypal. It is embedded in who we are, for we are marked by the crafting hand of God, who made us in his image. But we are also forged by the folly of our flight to human autonomy.

Present day culture has taken up this foolish flight and has made it a maxim for true happiness. The more independent we are, free from the constraints of the past, the church, and the demands of others, the more our life will soar towards fulfillment. Soar we may. But it's a directionless flight. And more frequently, it is not a flight at all. We simply limp our way along from one mirage to another.

The solution of course is not to embrace the bondage of the past, nor the failures of the church in history, but to return to the stern, but gracious Word of God, where we are invited to explore

177

and to enter into a very different understanding and experience of freedom.

Claude de la Colombiere in one pithy sentence goes to the heart of the matter: "submission to God's will frees us from all other yokes." And here lies the paradox of our existence, for we find this so hard to believe that we pursue the opposite. Freedom is freedom from all constraint, we believe. And true freedom involves flight from God, not submission to him.

We will never believe otherwise unless a deep conversion and transformation takes place at the core of our being. And here we are dependent on the illuminating work of the Holy Spirit, who helps us to see that God's "severe" way is the royal road to grace. That God's word leads us to righteousness. That being bound to God frees us from our own waywardness.

Free for God and free from our own folly, is the mystery of God's way. Free from our own wilfulness, we are free to receive all that God may give us. Free from the crippling bondage of sin, we become free to do God's good to others, and to our world.

Ultimately God's way is the way of love, the way of forgiveness, the way of welcome. God's way affirms our humanity because in the incarnation God himself became one of us and carried the whole weight of our sin in order to transform it by his healing love.

Reflection: In what way is God's way difficult for me?

OUR TRUE SELF

Put on the new self, created to be like God in true righteousness and holiness.

Ephesians 4:24

Pascal once made the comment: "we strive continually to adorn and preserve our imaginary self, neglecting the true one." One of the reasons for this folly is that we are people in defiance. We are guilty of a primordial flight from the presence of God. We believe that we are capable of single minded self-determination, and that this should shape our identity and destiny.

This self that we are creating is thus based on a negative. It does not come from a place of peace and connectedness, but from a tearing loose from the very center of our existence.

This imaginary self is the autonomous self. The self that is the product of our own achievements, but also of our deviousness, misuse of power, and greed. As a result, this is the never satisfied self. It always wants more. Enough is never enough.

But how do we become our true self? And what does that look like? This is made all the more difficult by the fact that our true self is not something we can find in the beauty of who we are, or somewhere under the rubble of our own making.

The true self is not like a deposit of gold that we can find in tons of excavation.

Since we are not inherently good and true, but have been formed by the folly of our flight, the true self can only come into being through painful transformations. No single conversion is sufficient. Not even our initial experience of the redemptive work of Christ through the Holy Spirit. That is merely the beginning and not the end point.

But it is a crucial beginning, for it is the homecoming that fundamentally reorients us. It brings us back to the center that alone is life giving.

The true self is the growing self that is formed and nurtured, not by its own achievements, but by the love of the Other. And no human other will suffice. Only the great Other revealed in the face of Jesus Christ can mark us with a love that is pure and deep enough to bring us to peace.

In communion with the community of the Trinity we discover a framework of relationships that empowers and makes us whole. And as a result of God's healing work in our lives, we can open ourselves to the gifts and blessings of others.

Other people, therefore, are no longer the ones to be feared, the ones to beat, but only people to love and to forgive.

Becoming who we were meant to be is not simply a growth in educational and vocational abilities. Nor is it only the development of relational skills. Much more fundamentally it is a growth in godliness and conformity to Jesus Christ.

It is in Christ, and in our growth in holiness, that we become who we were meant to be. But there is nothing instant and easy about this. It involves an on-going growth in grace. And it will involve an on-going conversion.

Reflection: In what ways are painful transformations still contributing to my journey towards wholeness.

SERVICE

LIVING LOVE OF NEIGHBOR

THE CHALLENGE
OF THE NEIGHBOR

Jesus replied: "'Love the Lord your God with all your heart and with all your soul and with all your mind.' This is the first and greatest commandment. And the second is like it: 'Love your neighbor as yourself.'"

Matthew 22:37-39

The work of God in our lives always involves a double movement: the vertical and the horizontal. The upward movement is drawing near to God in worship, prayer, and meditation. The outward movement calls us to serve our brothers and sisters in Christ. It also calls us to serve the neighbor in love and humility as we seek to do God's good to them.

We constantly need to remind ourselves that these two movements belong together and should not be separated. But this, of course, is not to suggest that they are both the same. God alone should be worshipped, and the neighbor should be served. Yet, it is also true that in serving the neighbor we are bringing glory to God.

Simone Weil once made the comment that "to treat one's neighbor, who is in affliction, with love is something like baptizing him (or her)." Here we have the idea that serving the neighbor is in fact like administering one of the sacraments.

What we must avoid is the idea that the vertical alone—the practice of prayer—is a spiritual activity, while the horizontal—

183

the act of service—is simply the doing of social good. The former is held to have eternal value, while the latter merely achieves the temporal good.

This kind of thinking reflects a dualism which runs against the major themes of Scripture. While the Bible is very careful to distinguish the Creator from the creature, and does not call prayer the doing of good to the neighbor, the Bible does reflect an amazing integration.

One way in which this integration is expressed is in the vision that our love for God is also to be expressed in our love for the neighbor. Loving God *and* loving the neighbor is, in fact, the true love of God. The idea that one can love God and neglect one's neighbor is in fact a perversion of one's love for God.

One of the key biblical themes that develops this concept is the gospel teaching that what we have done to the one in need we have actually done to Christ himself.

This means that service is one of the spiritual disciplines, and that blessing the one in need is as much a form of spirituality as prayer is. Put differently, we may say that worship is a service to God, and helping the neighbor in need is a form of worship in that we seek to honor God by blessing the neighbor.

There is joy in service, just as there is joy in worship. In prayer we seek to draw close to God, but we also seek to bring the neighbor to God. Thus the vertical and horizontal, while not the same, belong together so that in all things God may be glorified and others may be blessed.

Reflection: How can I become a sacrament to the world?

FORGETFUL GENEROSITY

But when you give to the needy, do not let your left hand know what your right hand is doing, so that your giving may be in secret. Then your Father, who sees what is done in secret, will reward you.

Matthew 6:3-4

In many ways there is nothing simple about the art of receiving and that of giving. Both acts of relationships, that express mutuality and care, are fraught with difficulty. For some, receiving is difficult. This is particularly the case for those who think they need to be self-sufficient. Others find giving a problem, either because they themselves have so little to give or because, though they have much to share, they believe that others are unworthy of their generosity.

Giving is an art that needs to be done well, and should be laced, not only with a major dose of grace, but also with the blessing of simplicity and forgetfulness.

George MacDonald once wrote, "nothing comes to stink worse than a good deed hung up in the moonlight of the memory."

So how then is it possible for us to give in good ways which makes generosity a blessing to others, but also to ourselves? I suggest that this becomes possible when we hold together a remembered generosity and the generosity of forgetfulness.

Remembered generosity is the celebration of the acts of kindness of *others* towards *us*. It is living in the deep joy that so much has been given to us. Not only has God given us our very life, but in so many ways God has enriched our life by his grace through the

185

work of his Spirit. And in God's providential care, so many others have contributed to our well-being, growth, and development. In fact, we can say that all that we are has been given.

The generosity of forgetfulness is what we extend to others. We give and forget our own generosity. We help, give, share in times of crisis, but we also contribute to others in the long haul of their development and in their spiritual journey. Thus both spontaneity and carefulness should characterize our generosity towards others.

But giving and sharing ought to come from a free place, and from a grateful heart. It is, therefore, marked with joy and simplicity. It seeks to do good to the other, not by binding them in dependency or a legalized reciprocity, but by reminding them that the love God has also reached them.

This generosity, therefore, gives praise to God and rejoices in his goodness. It builds hope, faith, and love. It is a living reminder that we are not alone, but the arms of love are there to hold and to empower us.

Reflection: What can I celebrate in others' generosity to me? What can I do to bless others?

ADVOCACY

You trample on the poor and force him to give you grain. Therefore, though you have built stone mansions, you will not live in them; though you have planted lush vineyards, you will not drink their wine.

Amos 5:11

The God of the biblical story is the God who calls *all* to newness of life. Saint and sinner, rich and poor, oppressor and oppressed, are all invited to the banqueting table of God's grace. Ethnicity, social status, gender, and orientation are no barriers to God's invitation.

But God has a special concern for the vulnerable ones of the earth. He draws close to the oppressed. He hears the cry of the poor. The humble ones who know and acknowledge their need catch God's careful attention.

And so throughout the pages of the biblical story we see God's attentiveness to the vulnerable ones. The story of the Exodus demonstrates this. The social legislation for the poor in the Pentateuch exemplifies this. The cry of the prophets verifies this. The mission of Jesus to the outcasts of society embodies this.

Throughout the church's long march in history we see again and again its passion for the poor. The early Christians picked up discarded babies from the rubbish tips of the cities in the Roman Empire. Monasticism practiced hospitality to the poor. The Wesleyan Revival brought God's good news to the lower working classes. And in our day we need only think of William Booth,

Dorothy Day and Mother Teresa. And more particularly we may think of the way in which most of the church in the Third World is the church of the poor for the poor.

Sadly, much of the church in the First World is cloaked in a middle-class respectability where the passion for serving the poor is often a mere flickering flame. Its Christianity has become one of easy believism and consumerism. This hardly empowers the church to become a servant of the poor.

But the church which is faithful to the biblical story is a church that serves the poor. How it does this is a constant challenge. There is no one way to serve the poor.

One of the ways to serve the poor is to join the poor and to advocate on their behalf. William Stringfellow notes that the church "is called as the advocate of every victim of the rulers of the age." What this means is that the community of faith is to take up the issues of the poor, and prophetically to call those who oppress or neglect the poor to accountability and transformation.

To be a good advocate requires much more than having a loud voice. The true advocate has entered into the pain of the poor through identification and solidarity. The advocate has walked a common road, has listened, and knows the heart cry and issues of the poor.

Out of these forms of identification the advocate seeks to be the voice of the poor to those in power who have chosen to turn a blind eye. While in the Third World the pain of the poor is often due to oppression, in the First World it is frequently due to neglect.

Advocacy is no secular strategy. It is a repetition of the heartbeat of God.

Reflection: Identification and advocacy—how do we more fully enter this difficult journey?

RESISTANCE

Then the Lord said to Moses, "Go to Pharaoh and say to him, 'This is what the Lord, the God of the Hebrews says: "Let my people go, so that they may worship me."'"

Exodus 9:1

While at times the basic stance of the church in society has been the folly of withdrawal, and at other times the weakness of compromise, its stance should be one of resistance in order to transform. Thus resistance should not be seen as being reactionary. And resistance is not the mere saying of "no." It's saying "no" in order to say "yes."

M.K. Gandhi gave much attention to the nature of resistance in the form of non-violent non-cooperation. He states, "I won't hate you when you are wrong nor will I obey you. Do what you like, but I will match my capacity to suffer against your capacity to inflict that suffering. [I will match] my soul force against your physical force and I will wear you down with good will."

It is obvious that this kind of resistance has a deep spiritual center. It recognizes the power of right against the weakness of wrong, even though in physical terms right is weak and wrong seems so strong. Moreover, this kind of resistance has the conversion and transformation of the oppressor in view.

This approximates the logic of the gospel. It is not unlike the mission of Jesus who in love engages his enemies seeking their conversion. But there are also differences in Gandhi's position with that of the biblical witness. The most fundamental is that

189

Christ takes upon himself the sin of the other in order to bring about an inner transformation.

So how then may the community of faith offer resistance to our world in the light of the biblical witness and Gandhi's strategy? There are a range of possibilities, none of which are easy, and none of which will leave the church untouched. In other words, the church's resistance to the worldliness of the world will deeply mark the church with the pain of the cross.

First of all, resistance cannot occur from a safe place. It can only come from the place of engagement. It is the church in the world carrying the world's sorrows and pain that can resist, and not the church in withdrawal.

Secondly, resistance must come from contemplation. It is easy to be negative. It is frequent that we are reactionary. It is often that we only see the bad and fail to see the good. As a result, our resistance may be at the wrong point. Resistance is a fruitless activity if it does not come from careful discernment.

Thirdly, resistance is the reverberation of God's "no" in order that God's "yes" may be heard. It is never the mere "no, this is wrong." It is much more "the ways of death must be abandoned and the rivers of life embraced." Resistance is not taking a detour. It is, instead, an entering into the realities of life with a different vision, and praying and working towards its realization.

Finally, the work of resistance is the labor of pain. One wins no friends in this engagement. For the conservative one is too radical. For the radicals one is not radical enough. The Kingdom of God falls neither in right or left ideological categories. It falls in-between. It falls to the left of the right and to the right of the left.

Rather than the piety of quietism, the flight of withdrawal, or the power to impose, Christian resistance has to do with the in-breaking of the Kingdom of God, and the turning away from the idols of our time.

Reflection: In Western churches do we know what a spirituality of resistance is all about, and what are its contours and pains?

THE WOUNDED HEALER

Praise be to the God and Father of our Lord Jesus Christ, the Father of compassion and the God of all comfort, who comforts us in all our troubles, so that we can comfort those in any trouble with the comfort we ourselves have received from God.

2 Corinthians 1:3-4

Our Western culture has become enamoured with the images of power, control, and self-sufficiency. These ideas have also found their way into the church sanctuary. Much Christian thinking and action revolve around these same ideas.

But these ideas are a far cry from the heart of the gospel. Self-sufficiency is to be replaced with dependence upon God, the ongoing work of his Spirit, and the joy of communal interdependence. The need for control is to be converted into the ability to be open and flexible, and to live in trust and vulnerability. And power for ourselves is to be replaced with a willingness to serve and empower others.

So it is simply not true that we can best bless and serve others when we are in the place of strength. The place of weakness and vulnerability is more frequently the place from which we have more to give to others. Henri Nouwen is, therefore, right that "our wounds ... (can) become sources of hope to others."

He is not suggesting that our festering inner hurts can be a source of help and hope to others. If we have those, then we need help and healing ourselves. We can hardly serve others well out of a place of anger, fear, unforgiveness, or bitterness.

But we can offer to others our own struggles and difficulties. Thereby, we cement the commonality of our humanity and the common journeys we all must make towards maturity, growth, and wholeness.

Sometimes, in sharing our own struggles we can give the other person a window into what may be happening to them. This is particularly helpful when they may have unrealistic ideas about themselves or others, or when they burden themselves with totally unrealistic expectations.

But the sharing of our woundedness should never be to draw attention to ourselves or to burden the other person. Instead, this sharing should once again point us all to the God of hope and healing. It should invite us to embrace the mystery of suffering, while at the same time drawing us into a deeper trust in the God of all grace and mercy.

Thus in humility we can give ourselves to others, not simply through sharing our giftedness, blessings, and resources, but also our own needs, struggles, and fears.

Reflection: In what way do I make myself available to others in vulnerability?

PROCLAIM AND LIVE JUBILEE!

Consecrate the fiftieth year and proclaim liberty throughout the land to all its inhabitants. It shall be a jubilee for you; each of you is to return to his family property and each to his own clan.

Leviticus 25:10

It is most curious that the Bible is often regarded as an outmoded and therefore irrelevant book, and that we moderns are somehow ethically and morally superior. The forward and upward movement of history, it is claimed, has left the past in its wake, just like a speedboat soon reduces a dingy to the far horizon.

But then suddenly, as in the present day Jubilee movement to forgive Third World debt, biblical categories become relevant once more to many people in the general community.

It seems foolish to me to elevate the present over the past as if we have it all together. Moreover, to consign the past to the dustbin is sheer *hubris*. And this is all the more foolish when we are no longer willing to listen to the enduring texts of the Old Testament.

The concept of Jubilee is an important Old Testament notion. It recognizes that in a clan culture based on land ownership, use, and productivity, it was nevertheless possible for people to become disinherited, marginalized and exploited. This highlights a reoccurring social problem that there seems to be no *one* social system that guarantees fairness and equality for all.

But this should never be accepted as the inevitability of circumstance and history. Exploitation and injustice should always be resisted and overcome.

This is the picture that is set out in the Old Testament. Jubilee is simply one of the many provisions which has the poor in view and champions their liberation and freedom. As such, Jubilee reflects something of the very heart of Yahweh. God is not simply concerned about the poor, but works for their redemption and provision.

Jubilee, while particular to the Old Testament, has echoes in the New Testament. The blessing of the poor, their welcome to the banqueting table, and the notion that serving the poor means serving Christ, are all indicators that God's heart for the oppressed and marginalized is as passionate as ever.

Sharon Ringe notes that "the Jubilee traditions highlight the fact that in Christ people are met by the healing, freeing, redeeming presence of God at their points of greatest pain."

Jubilee is not a good idea. It is to be a practice. Its key notion is to give back, and to empower those who have experienced deprivation. This calls the giver to a spirituality of generosity and relinquishment. It may mean opening our hand even to the cost of ourselves. Jubilee is not giving in order to achieve a surplus, but a fundamental restoration in terms of basic human need.

Reflection: In what ways do I need to be converted in order to practice Jubilee?

WITNESS

SACRAMENTS FOR A BROKEN WORLD

THE WILLING WITNESS

"You are the light of the world. A city on a hill cannot be hidden ... In the same way, let your light shine before men, that they may see your good deeds and praise your Father in heaven."

Matthew 5:14-16

Christianity is fundamentally a missionary religion. The God of the Bible as Creator has the whole of the cosmos in view. And despite the particularity of God's covenant with Israel, the Jewish people were called to be a light to the nations living in covenant faithfulness to the God of the Exodus.

With the death and resurrection of Christ, and the outpouring of the Holy Spirit, this global theme becomes more evident. The good news is that all may hear and rejoice in the mighty works of God.

God's passionate concern for all, particularly the vulnerable ones of the earth, is a concern that the church has sometimes borne with persevering zeal, but at other times with trifling neglect.

Particularly in our day, the work of witness has become problematical. This is due not only to the cultural captivity of the church, but also to the relativism that pluralism has brought to the reality of the work and life of the church. We have at best become reluctant and uncertain witnesses to the love and grace of God in Christ Jesus.

The recovery of a life of witness will hardly occur through the adoption of techniques or motivations sculpted by guilt. It can only come through a recovery of a deeper life with God, and a different stance towards our neighbor.

D. T. Niles in speaking of evangelism as "a beggar telling another beggar where both could find something to eat" points the way for a different stance towards the neighbor who is outside of the community of faith. So often, we wrongly have the idea that our witness should come out of strength, certainty, and having our life all sorted out. Yet witness should come from a very different place which will empower us in our witness.

This different place may be understood as being fellow travelers, where the one is able to share with another the purpose and final goal of the journey—life in the presence of God. Or, we are all on a journey towards greater wholeness, and the one shares with another that this is found in the healing embrace of God in Christ.

Witness should occur in the normal places we inhabit—the home, the neighborhood, school, the marketplace, and in our recreational activities. It is *not* trying to be something special for God. It is simply being ourselves and being present to and hospitable towards others. It is not doing something special, it is rather the overflow of a life lived with God empowered by his Spirit.

Here, word and deed complement each other. Proclamation and service become the twin voices of the people of God.

Reflection: How can I be more fully with others so that my witness becomes a more normal part of my life?

A SIGN OF THE KINGDOM

The creation waits in eager expectation for the sons of God to be revealed ... in hope that the creation itself will be liberated from its bondage to decay and brought into the glorious freedom of the children of God.

Romans 8:19-21

Even though some of the early Church fathers spoke of Christians being the third race, in every way Christians are the same as other people. They too, come crying into the world and whimper their way to the sunset of their life's journey. They too, remain single or marry; do great exploits or live a mediocre existence. Serve others well, but fail in many ways.

Yet, in another way Christians are called to be very different. David Bosch expresses this eschatologically: Christians are to be "a fragment of the world to come."

This is both a wonderful invitation, and a huge challenge at the same time. For it means that we are invited to be different in the midst of the daily affairs and realities of life in order that we may be witnesses to the Kingdom of God.

To be a Christian means that one has been impacted and transformed by the work and words of Christ by his Spirit. The living presence of Christ means that one is constantly reminded and reoriented to experience and to live the values of the Kingdom of Heaven—values that were so evidently embodied in all that Jesus was, said and did.

These values of love of God, service to the neighbor, reconciliation, the work of peace, the power of healing, resisting idolatry, the practice of justice, and the celebration of God's *shalom,* are to be woven by the Spirit into the very texture of our being, and also into the communities of faith of which we are a part.

While we will never fully embody these values as Jesus did, we have been impacted by these values, and they are to grow in us like ripening fruit. This growth will be sustained in prayer, word, sacrament, celebration and service, but above all by God's empowering presence with us.

These values, surprisingly, are not simply values for the here and the now. They are the values of eternity. The fundamental difference is that in the age to come they will come to full fruition.

The great mission of the people of God, therefore, is to be a witness, not only to what the Spirit of God is doing amongst us, but also to what God's final future will be like.

Thus, Christians in the midst of the world live at the edge of eternity. They embody the Kingdom of God, and witness to its full coming. Thus they constantly point beyond themselves to what God will yet do.

Reflection: In what ways can I anticipate more of God's future in my present circumstances?

GOD AND WORLD

My prayer is not that you take them out of the world, but that you protect them from the evil one.

John 17:15

Throughout the church's long march in history the church's attitude towards its engagement with the world has been a varying one. Sometimes, the church has accented the theme of withdrawal. At other times, the church has become almost submerged in the world. In better times, the church has seen itself as God's agent for change and transformation.

These varying themes take on particular urgency as I pen these words in the city of Yangon, Myanmar, where the church is struggling with its complicit silence in a country run by a military dictatorship. Between silence, on the one hand, and prophetic witness, on the other, often lie the blood of martyrs.

Karl Rahner once pointed out that sometimes we have made "God worldless," while at other times we have made "the world godless." This is a serious distortion in both directions since we need to see God as present to the world and the world as being called into the presence of God.

While every form of deism absents God from the world, every form of pantheism submerges God into the world so that the distinction between God and world is lost.

The biblical picture of the relationship between God and the world is amazingly dialectic and richly textured. Here every

201

simplistic categorization falls silent before the mosaic of God's engagement with the world he has made.

God exists independent of and before the world was called into being. But God's revelation of himself is intimately connected with the world shaped from chaos into a harmony ordered by the will of God. While God remains wholly other, he unfolds himself in his world. Its beauty, order, and awesomeness, reflect something of the greatness of God's creative activity.

In the creation of humankind we can particularly see the power of God's handiwork. Made in God's image, humans exercise dominion in the created order and further shape the world that God has made. Thus while the heavens declare the glory of God and all of nature sings the praises of God, humankind is invited to live in God and for God so that all of life may reflect God's *shalom* and majesty.

Ultimately the world cannot be godless for its very reality is due to God's shaping hand and is sustained by God's generous care. Nor can God be worldless because God has made all things and all things depend on him.

If God and world were to be wholly separated, then God is no longer the creator and the God of history, and the world would fall into chaos. God's love for the world continues to be the world's basis for hope and renewal. The world's love for God makes the world truly dependent on him who sustains all in all.

Reflection: A world without God is a world without a true center and a true hope. A world with God is a world of hope. Where in the world do we need a recovery of this hope?

A WIDE VISION OF ACTION

For God was pleased to have all his fullness dwell in him, and through
him to reconcile to himself all things, whether things on earth or things
in heaven, by making peace through his blood, shed on the cross.

Colossians 1:19-20

There is nothing skimpy about God's concern and action in the
world. The broad sweep moves from creation to recreation
and to new heavens and new earth. God as Creator and Redeemer
sustains all that has been made and calls humanity to partake of
his redemptive love.

God's love and concern embraces our reconciliation to him,
the building of communities of faith, the work for justice and
the responsible stewardship of all creation. Nothing falls outside
of God's recreating activity: soul and body, individual and
community, spirituality and politics, and work and Sabbath.

Since God's action encompasses the whole human condition with
all its creativity, potentiality, idolatry and pain, our cooperation
with God involves a similar wide vision of action. As Christians,
we can't be reductionistic and emphasize only the soul and
spiritual concerns. God's grace and empowerment is for all of life,
not simply for a particular ministry.

Evelyn Underhill notes well that our ministry includes "the
ceaseless self-offering of the enclosed nun to the creation of beauty
or the clearance of slums." While we could readily emphasize other
roles in life: family care giver, community worker, priest, business
person or town planner, the point is the same—cooperation with

the Sovereign Lord draws us into the many and various arenas of life to serve the King in the midst of our daily activities.

Not surprisingly, the incessant question of many Christians, is whether all of these activities are of equal validity and carry the same priority. There are a number of ways to approach this complex issue. The first, is simply to note that in life we carry multiple duties and fulfill multiple roles: mother and business person; elder and artist. Secondly, God does call the individual person to a particular major role: clergy person, politician, teacher or missionary. Thirdly, the diversity of God's action can only be borne and carried forward into the world by the local community of faith. And in many instances, it can only be carried by the church as a whole in a particular country, and sometimes, only by the church globally.

We need to be careful that the breath and width of God's mission does not immobilize us because we feel we have to do it all and become overwhelmed. God's will always calls us to particularity: a place, a neighborhood, a people. But in seeking to serve them well we are invited to join hands with others in solidarity and partnership.

Reflection: In the broad sweep of God's mission what role do I play?

UNDERSTANDING OUR WORLD

For the foolishness of God is wiser than man's wisdom, and the weakness of God is stronger than man's strength.

1 Corinthians 1:25

There are some Christians who believe that it is only important for us to understand God and his Word. Nothing else, according to them really matters.

In one sense, these brothers and sisters in the faith are right. To know God, and to worship, and obey him is our highest good and joy. But in an other way, I disagree with this perspective. We should not only know and understand God, but also ourselves and the world in which we live. It is this latter point in particular that I wish to explore further.

We are very much in the world and shaped by its values. In fact, the more unaware we are of this, the more we are influenced by our culture. For some, it is the experience of living in another culture that begins to make them aware of the cultural values that their home country has given them. For others, it is the experience of failure or disappointment that forces them to question aspects of their implicit worldview. For other people, it is joining with the marginalized that causes them to question aspects of the dominant culture.

There is a very good reason why Christians need to understand the dominant ethos of their culture. And the main reason, is not in order to be effective in evangelism, even though that is very important. The further important reason is, that if we are not aware of both the good aspects of our culture as well as its idolatries and dysfunctionalities, then we easily make our culture the determinant for the way we read Scripture and order our lives.

In other words, we read the unquestioned aspects of our worldview into Scripture. As a result, it is our culture that then determines our values, rather than the Scriptures that we read and embrace. It hardly needs saying that it should be the other way round. It is Scripture that should critique culture; not culture that should determine the way we read Scripture.

And there is much in our contemporary culture that needs serious questioning: narcissistic individualism over cooperation, productivity over personhood, the material over the spiritual, war-making over peace-making, and the powerful over the weak. Paul Tounier puts it this way: "A grave crisis has overtaken this civilization of ours, which has asserted the primacy of logic over intuition, of the scientist over the artist, of technology over human beings, of the logician over the believer, of the committee of experts over life."

We are called, therefore, to a double task: to know God and to know our world. More specifically, we are called to understand our world in the light of God's wisdom. And further still, we are invited not simply to understand our world, but work for its transformation through the coming of God's Kingdom amongst us.

This calls us not only to prayer, but also to evangelization and the work for justice.

Reflection: Are there ways in which I need to become more aware of the values of our age?

LIVING THE GOSPEL

Neither circumcision nor uncircumcision means anything; what counts is a new creation.

Galatians 6:15

One does not begin by living the gospel, but first by receiving the gospel. God does not come to us first with a demand, but with a gift.

This gift of new life in Christ through the Spirit comes as the surprise of God. For some it comes in the normal rhythms of life, for others at critical junctures in their life's journey, and for others again in the moments of crisis or despair.

While this is no forced gift, there is little doubt that God prepares us for the gift of new life. For we are so wrapped up in our own ways, abilities and achievements, and are so blinded, that we can't see the true meaning and purpose of life. So, we have to be awakened to see what God wants to give. We have to be made aware of our need for God's grace. We have to be taught how to open our hands and our hearts.

Receiving the gospel is receiving God's welcome. It is receiving the Spirit. It is enjoying forgiveness. It is embracing salvation in Christ.

This new life that God gives is no addendum to our life. It is not the appendix to the book of life, and certainly not a mere footnote on one of its pages. God wants it to be the main story!

But it has to become this in our life. God's new life has to grow in us. God's new story of love and forgiveness has to replace our old story. And that old story continues with its claims that clamor to be heard and its desire to dominate.

As God's story increasingly becomes our story and God's ways become a part of who we are, then we are beginning to live the gospel. Receiving the gospel is to renew us. Living the gospel is to worship God and bless others.

And we can more fully bless others when God's story becomes our heartbeat and passion. This is beautifully expressed by Cardinal Sunhard: "to be a witness does not consist in engaging in propaganda ...but in being a living mystery. It means to live in such a way that one's life would not make sense if God did not exist."

Living the gospel is not a matter of a technique that seeks to convert others. It is simply the opening out to others of a life that has been opened to God. Or to put that differently, it is revealing the awakening that God has brought to our lives.

Living the gospel is living God's main story of the redemption of Christ for humanity and the created order in the particularities of our daily lives and relationships, while acknowledging that so much of the old story still persists.

Reflection: In what ways may God's story increasingly become my own?

AN AFTERWORD

LIVING THE TENSIONS
OF LIFE AND FAITH

So how does one live this dialectic between ecstasy and routine? How do we live well the creative tension between moments of inspiration and the mundaneness of our existence? How do we live the vision of the Kingdom of God in the midst of the daily round of duties and responsibilities?

There is only one answer: with difficulty.

There are some obvious reasons why this is so. The main one being, that a life of faith, touched by the Spirit's brooding and empowering presence lived in the challenges and ambiguities of daily life, knows no simple straight lines. Nothing in this journey is self-evident. Nothing is predictable. It is full of surprises. It is full of God's grace, and our failure. It is walking clearly ahead, and stumbling along.

Given that both the heavenly vision and mundane existence are part of the Christian's life of faith in the world, how are these two realities inter-related?

Here we see some differing options.

For some only the heavenly vision is important. That is seen as real life! The daily realities of life are seen as secondary. They are an interruption. This thinking reflects a dualistic spirituality, and leads to a world-denying form of Christianity.

A sad variation on this theme is that some people get upset and angry that the heavenly vision does not predominate. Thus they feel that God has let them down. They become disillusioned about the life of faith. Because they think that life should always be good, they become discouraged when difficulty, hardship, or suffering come their way.

At the other end of the continuum is the cynical Christian. For such a person, the moments of inspiration are so rare, and the mundane reality of their life is so all pervasive, that the life of faith has virtually become delusional. Why pray, they say, when nothing seems to change. And why relate to this occasional and absent God? It is better, they say, to celebrate our humanity, and embrace the secularity of the world.

In between these two perspectives—only heavenly realities or only secularity is worthwhile—lie other options. These I believe reflect more adequately the vision of the biblical story.

God is present. He is also hidden. We do catch glimpses of the Kingdom of God, and we do live in a real world where the presence of God seems often to be absent.

What this invites us to embrace and live, is the theological vision that the wisdom of God, and the way of the Spirit, are to shape the way we live our life in the world.

The heartbeat of the gospel, the way of love, the imitation of Christ, the life of prayer, are to inform our values, and determine the choices we make. These shape the way we live our relationships, create and sustain family, relate to neighbors, and involve ourselves in the world of business, the arts, and politics.

Thus we don't pine away when we only have glimpses of the heavenly vision, the renewing work of the Spirit, and the moments of ecstasy. Instead, we carry these as sacred seed into our daily lives.

The seeds of the Kingdom of God within us become the inspiration and imagination of all we seek to do in life. And while that vision may dim, and while the ordinariness of life may overtake us, and the secularity of our world may erode the life of faith, we are called to ongoing renewal, and to find bread for the journey.

Just because ordinariness may predominate, this does not mean that the mundaneness of our existence is determinative. The occasional moments of revelation, sense of God's presence, movement of the Spirit, can be the fuel for the long journey of faith in the realities of daily life.

Thus the whispers from the edge of eternity are the seedbed for a life of faith, reflection, worship, and service.

INDEX OF SCRIPTURE
REFERENCES

OLD TESTAMENT

Genesis 12:1, **161**
Genesis 15:1, **47**
Genesis 29:20, **93**
Exodus 9:1, **189**
Leviticus 25:10, **93**
1 Samuel 3:10, **111**
1 Samuel 16:10-12, **77**
2 Chronicles 7:14, **85**
Psalm 23:1-3a, **155**
Psalm 30:11-12, **57**
Psalm 42:1-2, **99**
Psalm 42:5, **39, 61, 165**
Psalm 42:11, **55**
Psalm 51:6, **107**
Psalm 55:7-8, **117**
Psalm 89:14-15, **105**
Psalm 90:9, **169**
Psalm 90:10, **171**
Psalm 90:12, **173**
Psalm 95:6-7, **113**
Psalm 102:1-2, **45**
Psalm 104:14-15, **43**
Psalm 130:7, **59**
Proverbs 3:5-6, **51**
Proverbs 13:12, **63**
Proverbs 13:19a, **101**
Proverbs 30:7-8, **139**
Isaiah 42:1, **121**
Isaiah 45:3, **35**

Isaiah 55:1, **17**
Isaiah 53:5b, **127**
Isaiah 57:15, **87**
Jeremiah 2:13, **141**
Ezekiel 33:7, **103**
Ezekiel 37:5, **151**
Amos 5:11, **187**
Amos 7:14-15, **147**

NEW TESTAMENT

Matthew 5:14-16, **197**
Matthew 5:16, **75**
Matthew 5:43-44, **79**
Matthew 6:3-4, **185**
Matthew 9:17, **21**
Matthew 22:37-39, **183**
Mark 8:34, **153**
Mark 11:22-23, **31**
Luke 4:1-2, **135**
Luke 19:5, **115**
John 6:35, **119**
John 17:15, **201**
John 17:15-16, **95**
John 17:22-23, **89**
Acts 2:44-45, **71, 149**
Romans 6:13, **81**
Romans 6:22 , **177**
Romans 6:22-23, **25**
Romans 8:19-21, **199**

215

Romans 8:23, **175**
Romans 12:2a, **129**
Romans 15:5-6, **69**
Romans 15:28-29, **159**
1 Corinthians 1:25, **205**
1 Corinthians 12:12-13, **67**
2 Corinthians 1:3-4, **191**
2 Corinthians 1:6, **163**
2 Corinthians 2:15-16, **33**
2 Corinthians 4:5, **145**
2 Corinthians 5:1-2, **37**
2 Corinthians 8:9, **23**

Galatians 6:15, **208**
Ephesians 3:16-17a, **29**
Ephesians 4:22-24, **131**
Ephesians 4:24, **179**
Ephesians 5:1-2, **73**
Philippians 2:8, **49**
Colossians 1:19-20, **203**
2 Thessalonians 2:13, **19**
1 Timothy 4:9-10, **15**
James 5:16, **125**
1 Peter 2:9, **137**
1 John 3:16, **91**

INDEX OF AUTHORS
AND SOURCES

Barth, Karl, 141
Basil of Caesarea, 35
Bernanos, Georges, 59
Bernard of Clairvaux, 20
Bondi, Roberta, 57
Bonhoeffer, Dietrich, 32, 126, 146
Bosch, David, 199
Campbell, Joseph, 161
Chrysostom, John, 137
Courtenay, Bryce, 63
Day, Dorothy, 24, 32, 147
de Chardin, Teilhard, 17, 52
de la Colombiere, Claude, 178
Didache, The, 71
Dostoevsky, F., 92
Einstein, Albert, 129
Ellul, Jacques, 32
Eusebius, 95
Forsyth, P. T., 113
Francke, August Hermann, 32
Galilea, Segundo, 136
Gandhi, M. K., 189
Guardini, Roman, 165
Hauerwas, Stanley, 67
Hubmaier, Balthasar, 150
Hugo, Victor, 99, 171
Illich, Ivan, 151
James, William, 29
Julian of Norwich, 61
Kierkegaard, Soren, 40

lectio divina, 112
Lichtenberg, G. C., 159
MacDonald, George, 185
Malamud, Bernard, 55, 87
Manson, W., 175
Maritain, Jacques, 131
Meehan, Francis, 85
Merton, Thomas, 104, 153, 156
Mitterand, Francois, 173
Moltmann, Jürgen, 70
Mother Teresa, 32
Murray, Andrew, 50
Newbigin, Lesslie, 76
Niles, D. T., 198
Nouwen, Henri, 74, 117, 191
Pascal, Blaise, 179
Peterson, Eugene, 120
Pope John XXIII, 89
Rahner, Karl, 164, 201
Ringe, Sharon, 194
Rohr, Richard, 127
Romero, Oscar, 32
Saliers, Don, 107
St. Anselm, 48
St. Anthony, 45
St. Augustine, 101
St. Benedict, 78
St. Francis, 34
St. Irenaeus, 16
St. John of the Cross, 140

Stringfellow, William, **121, 188**
Sunhard, Cardinal, **208**
Tertullian, 37
Tibetan saying, **21**
Tounier, Paul, **206**
Underhill, Evelyn, **105, 203**

Vanier, Jean, **81, 116**
Weil, Simone, **183**
Wesley, John, 79
West, Morris, **43, 169**
Williams, Niall, **25**
Yeats, W. B. **94**

CPSIA information can be obtained at www.ICGtesting.com
Printed in the USA
BVOW05s0546161214

379491BV00001B/59/A